a Lancashire
Monastic Way

*a walk through Lancashire and
south Cumbria visiting sites of
medieval monastic houses*

By John Convey

Published by John Convey

First published February 2011

Reissued in this revised format 2016

ISBN 978-0-9954621-0-6

Email: John@conveys.org

Graphic Design by Dan Convey: enquire@danconveys.com

Any profits from the sale of this book will be donated to charity

Acknowledgements

I would like to thank the following for their help: in Preston, Dorothy MacLeod in the Local Studies Library, not only for providing sources but, along with her husband Andrew, reading through the script and making many useful suggestions; Ann Dennison in the Harris Library; library staff in the Ormskirk and Banks Trailer/Mobile libraries; Bruce Jackson and his staff in the Lancashire Record Office and Ken Davies and staff in the Lancashire County Archaeological Service. In Cumbria, thanks are due to the staff in the Cumbria Archives Service in Kendal. I thank my wife Eileen, and Dave Hemus, for reading the script and suggesting improvements, and John Moffat for proof-reading the final script.

The following were kind enough to allow me to publish my photographs taken on their property: Rev Chris Jones, Vicar of Ormskirk (Chapel of St John the Divine, Lathom and Lectern from Burscough Priory); Chantelle Seaborn, Property Manager Central Lancashire, National Trust (Rufford Old Hall); Rev Bill Sloan, Vicar of St Michael and All Angels, Hoole (St Michael's Church, Much Hoole); Fr Hoole (Ladyewell Shrine); David Porter, Partner, Knight Frank LLP, Manchester (St. Saviour's Chapel, Stydd); Head of Central Services, Whalley Abbey (Whalley Abbey); John Miller, Chief Executive, Heritage Trust for the North West, [who manage Sawley Abbey, which is owned by English Heritage] (Sawley Abbey); Rev Michael Roberts [who also donated an interior view of the church] (St Michael's Church, Cockerham); Barry Hutton, Customer Relations Advisor, First TransPennine Express (Carnforth Station); and Canon Robert Bailey, Vicar of Cartmel Priory Church (Cartmel Priory). Other images are reproduced with thanks to Lancashire County Library and Information Service (Gardiner's Almshouses).

Every effort has been made to ensure that all copyright holders have been contacted and agree to images being reproduced; we apologise if we have made any errors on this count, and will endeavour to correct these in any future edition.

The route maps are reproduced under Licence Number 100050377 from Ordnance Survey.

To my grandchildren
- the next generation of walkers

Contents

Introduction

Lancashire and south Cumbria are blessed with a wonderful variety of landscapes and seascapes, from the rolling hills and valleys of the Douglas and Ribble valleys, and flatter lands of the Fylde coast and Morecambe Bay, to the higher often wooded hills around Grange and Furness. This walk includes all of these different landscapes and seascapes in its quest to visit the remains or sites of many of the monastic houses which thrived in the Lancashire of medieval times; it also includes other places of note along the way, such as medieval hospitals, churches and chapels, of the 'old' county of Lancashire. Maybe there's an added advantage to visiting these churches and chapels along the way - according to a verse found in Llantysilio Church near Llangollen:

> "Every time I see a Church
> I pay a little visit
> So when at last I'm carried in
> The Lord won't say 'Who is it' "?

The original idea was to use, as far as possible, ancient routes which pilgrims and monks of old would have used, but as most of these are now under tarmac and busy with traffic, it seemed preferable to choose a route away from modern roads, using public footpaths along river banks and canal towpaths, or sections of established long-distance footpaths such as the Ribble Way, the Lancashire Coastal Path, the Cistercian Way and the Cumbria Coastal Way. The going is easy and so suitable for all ages and walking abilities; there's a bit of a climb out of Grange-over-Sands on the way to Cartmel (just over 200 metres in height), but otherwise the going for the most part is gentle, walking through contrasting and beautiful countryside, riverside and seaside, and one is never short of a wonderful view.

Part One, gives details of the walk itself, which is made up of two linear sections - Upholland to Sawley and Cockerham to Furness - and also gives a brief overview of each monastic house along the way; these overviews are incorporated into the text at the appropriate location. After so many centuries and so much research written on the monasteries, it is difficult to write much that is new, so most of the overviews are based on several recognised sources, both primary and secondary, with a few bits and pieces that might be new to some people. As these brief histories are only a start, for anyone wishing to dig deeper into the history of these monastic houses ....

Part Two gives a detailed list of sources of information, including website addresses where relevant. The more general sources are given in Appendix 1, and the other Appendices cover more particular sources for each individual monastic house. Appendix 1 includes information on library and archive catalogues and other sources from both local and national authorities, and sources such as the Victoria County History of Lancashire, books by Marshall, Knowles, Dugdale, and Tanner; the Valor Ecclesiasticus, and cartularies on several monasteries. Many of these sources could have been found using online catalogues, but it seemed a good idea to bring all the sources together for convenience and in case the Internet crashed! These sources, many annotated, are listed in reverse-chronological order of the original text, as far as is feasible, for at least two reasons: we would hope that more recent writings would include the most up to date information about new finds, both of documentary sources and of archaeological and other investigations; and because more recent writings will cite earlier works so the researcher can build up a comprehensive list of relevant sources over the centuries.

I set out to do a 'green' walk as far as possible, hence the information about buses and trains for each section. The beginning and end of each section is close to public transport, apart from the beginning of the Ribble Way, which is about 1.5 miles from buses at Longton. I cheated sometimes if my wife 'happened to be going my way' in the car! Helpful websites include http://www.traveline-northwest.co.uk/ and www.thetrainline.com, as well as the websites of individual companies, such as Stagecoach, Arriva, TransPennine Express, etc. Lancashire County Council's 'Mario' GIS system - http://mario.lancashire.gov.uk/viewer.htm - is invaluable for many things, including showing where bus stops are located! As well as paper maps, for a small annual fee online maps are available for printing on https://www.ordnancesurvey.co.uk/osmaps/.

Guide to using the book

Detailed description of the walk	-	begins with footprint icon
Histories of monastic houses	-	with blue background

The route of the walk is shown on the several Ordnance Survey maps as a black dotted line. These maps are 'Reproduced by permission of Ordnance Survey on behalf of HMSO. © Crown copyright 2011. All rights reserved. Ordnance Survey Licence Number 100050377.'

Part One
(the walk)

Upholland Priory to Sawley Abbey

1 Upholland Priory to Lathom Park Chapel
[10.5 miles]

Ordnance Survey map: **Explorer 285**
Public transport: buses to and from Wigan, Skelmersdale, Ormskirk,
Southport, etc in School Lane, Upholland. At Lathom, buses travel along the
nearby A5209 to Ormskirk, Parbold etc.

St Thomas the Martyr Church, Upholland, has a vibrant and very welcoming community today. Prayer continues still in the church as it has for around 700 years; and its history is reflected in those prayers - before Communion the congregation says:

"Gather your people from the ends of the earth to feast with Benedict, Thomas Becket and all your saints at the table in your kingdom."

It was the monks of the Benedictine order who were established here in 1319, and the priory named St Thomas the Martyr, just less than 150 years after the death of Thomas Becket. Robert de Holland was persuaded by the Bishop of Lichfield to convert a former college into a priory, with a prior and twelve monks.

Upholland Priory
OS Map Reference: SD 52290 05090
Access: Church St, Upholland, WN8 0ND.
Tel: (01695) 622895.
Phone or see website for services, etc
[http://www.stthomasthemartyr.org.uk]

In old records the spelling varies, to include Holande or Holland or Up Holland. The priory was never wealthy, and had problems at times owing to the monks' lifestyle and the condition of the buildings. Income was derived from the rectories of Childwall and Whitwick (in Leicestershire) among other sources. Towards the end of the fifteenth century the Bishop was told that the monks did not observe their rule and the church was in a state of disrepair. By the time of the Dissolution, the church had been repaired, there were just five monks including the prior, and all were priests, and there were 26 servants. The monks were living in separate bedchambers, with most of them sleeping on feather beds. It seems that the priory was not popular with the local community, but at the Dissolution it was supporting two old people, and two children at school, thus fulfilling one of the key duties of the monastic movement - helping the traveller, the stranger, the needy and the local community.

'The church has a Tardis-like effect - the interior is much larger than one would imagine from outside.'

Upholland Priory was one of the few places, like Cartmel Priory, where the priory church was not destroyed but preserved for use as a parish church for the local people. Today's nave was the chancel of the priory and was built in the fourteenth century, the present chancel being added in the nineteenth century. The tower is late fifteenth century, built while the monks were still in community here. The church has a Tardis-like effect - the interior is much larger than one would imagine from outside. The interior of the nave is quite magnificent for a small community of monks, Pevsner noting that 'the nave interior is unforgettable with its tall and slender piers'.

The priory buildings were located south of the church, and all that remains today is part of the western wall (at the rear of the Conservative Club car park). The building was of two storeys, with the monks' dormitory on the first floor. From the car park mentioned you can see a raised opening in the south aisle of the church which would have been a means of access from the priory build-ings to the church, possibly the 'night stairs'.

Inside the present church there is a model of how the priory buildings may have looked. Another link with the era of the monks is the 'Mary window', so called because it has an image of Jesus' mother Mary in the centre; this was made up of fragments of medieval stained glass found in the grounds of the priory - the window was paid for by all the Marys in the village. (For sources of information on the priory see Appendix 1 and Appendix 2).

An excellent place to start a walk, or a pilgrimage!

Map: 1-1

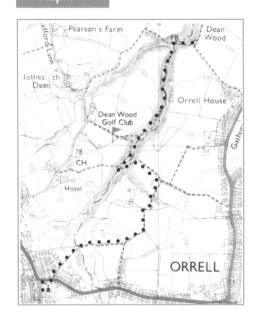

[1-1] From the priory church, turn right up School Lane. Derby House is on the right, dated 1633, with the Stanley crest; it was formerly called the Old Manor Court House. After a short distance take the public footpath between buildings on the left (Back School Lane); this path leads between houses, over the end of Priory Nook and out into fields in a north-easterly direction.

Cross the footbridge over Dean Brook, and walk across the golf course (you shouldn't get hit as the path is parallel to fairways - but beware anyway!). When you reach the edge of the golf course, take the track almost opposite (there is a way-mark).

Follow this track (look straight ahead for a view of Winter Hill, living up to its name with snow in March 2010) until it turns towards the farm, then take the path in a north-easterly direction over a brook, and passing a pond on the right.

At the next junction, take the left hand path towards the woods. Steps have been provided down into the ravine; cross

over the footbridge and immediately turn right and follow Dean Brook (from now on there is a load of lovely black mud for much of the path along the brook; also beware fallen trees across the path!).

[1-2]. Cross over two footbridges, then when you reach the next footbridge, take the right-hand path - you can see ahead steps made in the side of the ravine. Half way up the steps, there is a way-marked path to the left; or climb up to the top of the ravine, over a stile and into a field; turn left along the edge of the field.

"If you're lucky, you may hear a woodpecker at work. Care needs to be taken along the path, as in parts it is not well maintained - muddy, sloping and slippery."

After the length of the first field, the path dives down into the ravine again, meeting the path on the side of the ravine near a fallen tree. If you're lucky, you may hear a woodpecker at work. Care needs to be taken along the path, as in parts it is not well maintained - muddy, sloping and slippery.

Keep to this path, and don't head down towards the brook. When you reach the end of the wood and the river Douglas, take the track to the right alongside the Douglas (if you go left you end up tantalisingly short of a footbridge - which is on private property).

Follow the track under the M6 and alongside the railway until you reach the road at Gathurst. (From here you can catch a train on Southport-Wigan-Manchester line, or a local bus to Wigan, Shevington, etc.)

Map: 1-2

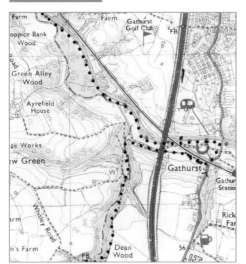

The pub by the canal quite understandably used to be called 'The Navigation'; more recently its name has changed surprisingly to the 'Baby Elephant'!

Map: 1-3

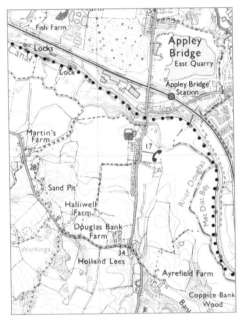

The towpath between Gathust and Appley Bridge is quite wide and firm, so suitable for wheelchairs and pushchairs, etc. Along this stretch the river Douglas (or Asland) can be seen on the left; in the days before the canal, the river was navigable from here to the sea, carrying mainly coal from Wigan; on Yates' map there is marked what is presumably a towpath on the east side of the river from here on.

You soon reach Dean Locks, where the oldest motorway (the canal) passes underneath the newer motorway (the railway) and then the newest motorway (the M6). It is a very pleasant walk up the Douglas Valley, in spite of the occasional pong from local industry; you see fields and woods on gently rising land, with the spires of Parbold in the distance. [1-3]

You pass Appley Locks, where a spare set of locks was created to deal with the large flow of traffic in each direction. [1-4] At Gillibrand Bridge (No 40), there is a footpath to the left towards Prior's Wood. Prior's Wood Hall (SD 50158 09616) -

"Priors Wood...on the south bank of the river Douglas about 1/2 mile from the site of Old Douglas Chapel.....
"There are evidences of a 16th or early 17th century dwelling..." some portions of the present house are probably of that period, considerable alterations and additions having been made during the present century....There is a generally accepted tradition that Prior's Wood was at one time associated in some way with the Priory of Upholland and so derived its name ....".

(Trans Lancs & Ches Hist Soc Vol 15 NS 1899 219).

Map: 1-4

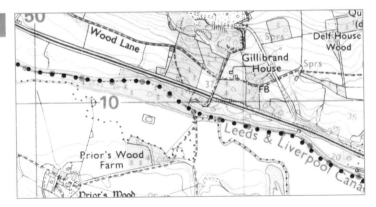

Cross at site of Douglas Chapel

Back on the canal, after a short time you are given an unusual gift - a bench! If you stay too long (or long enough?), the local mallards come always hopeful for food. At the next bridge, Chapel House Bridge, take a detour down the lane to the left between the Old School House and Chapel House Barn (it is a public footpath) and you will find on the left a cross marking the site of the medieval Douglas Chapel (SD 49783 10189). [1-5]

The Chapel, dedicated to St Mary, dated back to at least the thirteenth century, being rebuilt about 1620; it was thus older than Upholland Priory. It was finally demolished in 1878, or in 1875 according to the base of the cross which has stood on the site of the old chapel since 1906. The chapel may have been built by the Knights Hospitallers, and its later patrons were the Lathoms of Parbold. The chapel was a low, simple building of stone, with no tower or spire. The interior looked a little cramped, with six substantial columns supporting the roof; there was a stained glass window donated in 1621 at the time of rebuilding, and a gallery for singers accessed, it is believed, by a flight of stairs on the exterior of the chapel (similar to St Saviour's, Stydd).

The pulpit and font were moved to Parbold's new church of Christ Church on Parbold Hill, and the chapel bell to the new schools, also on Parbold Hill. In the days before car boot sales, the chapel had a novel way of raising money - charity sermons! One Saturday in July 1837 the Rev T Bibby from Liverpool preached sermons morning and afternoon in support of Parbold Sunday School, and raised £29-4s-6d (which in today's money would be well over £2,000!). On the pedestal of the cross is inscribed:

"Here stood Old Douglas Chapel for four full centuries loved and thronged by those who worshipped God from all the country round. Existed 1526. Rebuilt 1621. Demolished 1875". (For sources of information on the Douglas Chapel see Appendix 1).

Nearby you will find Christ Church, Parbold (http://www.christchurchparbold.co.uk/), Church of Our Lady & All Souls, Parbold(http://www.ourladysparbold.org.uk/); and the Church of St Michael, Dalton (http://www.stmichaelsdalton.co.uk/).

Walk along the towpath to Parbold and its sawn-off windmill. Shortly after Parbold, we say goodbye to our companion the river Douglas, as it passes under the canal and winds its way north to the river Ribble. [1-6]

Canal peace in early spring

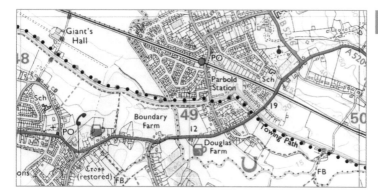

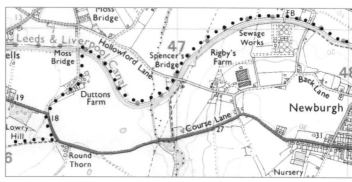

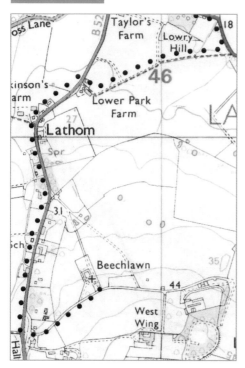

At Moss Bridge, the bridge after Spencer's Swing Bridge, take the lane south passing Dutton's Farm and join the main road. Turn left and walk along the main road for a short while (beware, as the road is busy and there is no footpath), and as the road bends to the left, take the marked footpath on the right. [1-7]

Walk diagonally across the field towards another stile, walk alongside a drainage channel, head straight ahead to the farm buildings (Lower Park Farm) and out onto the road. Turn left up the main road (there is a pavement, but there is no convenient alternative to this busy and noisy road) as far as the main entrance to Lathom Park. Turn left and make your way to the Chapel of St John the Divine at Lathom, along with the old almshouses, and Cromwell's Stone; Lathom Park with Lathom House is on the right. From here you can enjoy pleasant views towards Parbold hill. [Total miles to date = 10.5]

2 Lathom Chapel to Rufford via Burscough Priory
[8.5 miles]

Ordnance Survey map: **Explorer 285**

Public transport: at Lathom, buses travel along the nearby A5209 to Ormskirk, Parbold etc. For Burscough Priory, there is a bus stop on the A59 at the end of Abbey Lane (half mile walk from the priory), with buses to Ormskirk, Burscough, etc. Train stations at Burscough Bridge (approx 2 mile walk) for trains to/from Southport, Manchester, Wigan; and at Burscough Junction (approx just under 2 mile walk) for trains to/from Preston, Liverpool, Ormskirk. At Rufford, buses travel on the A59 to Ormskirk, Tarleton, etc, and also to Southport. Rufford train station is on the Ormskirk - Preston line..

Lathom Park Chapel
OS Map Reference: SD 45677 09399

Access: it is still in use as a chapel. (For services, etc see http://www.ormskirkparishchurch.org.uk/page.php?Page=31). The Chapel is open on Saturday and Sunday afternoons, 2.30 - 4.30pm, in the summer. Tel: (01695) 572143 (Ormskirk Parish Church)

This lovely little chapel was established in 1500, along with the almshouses adjoining. It was founded by Thomas Lord Stanley, the 2nd Earl of Derby, (possibly in thanksgiving for benefits received after the Battle of Bosworth) for a priest and eight bedesmen (persons who are paid to pray for the soul of another - OED).

It was used as a place of worship for tenants from the area from its beginning, and is still in use today for worship. This quiet, rural foundation has been at the centre of national affairs in its time: it either managed to escape suppression at the Dissolution of the monasteries,

or was refounded soon afterwards, the sanctuary screen incorporates parts of a Perpendicular original believed to have come from Burscough Priory, as did the oak eagle lectern; some bullet holes are visible in the sanctuary screen, being damaged during the famous siege of nearby Lathom House in 1644 during the Civil War, when the Countess of Derby withstood the might of Cromwell's army.

(For sources of information on the Chapel see Appendix 1 and Appendix 3).

[2-1] Starting from Lathom Chapel, return to Hall Lane passing the gate pier and octagonal Ormskirk

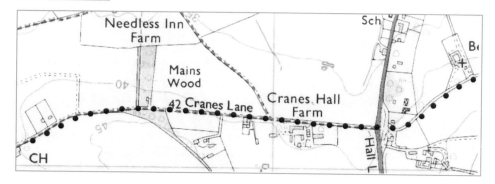

Lodge, go straight across to Cranes Lane, (initially wet and uneven but later you reach a tarmaced surface), passing Cranes Hall and Ormskirk Golf Club.

It is quite probable that this road was used by the family at Lathom House travelling to Burscough Priory. [2-2] At the junction, turn right up Sandy Lane; a Keeper's Lodge is on the right at the junction. At the next junction, turn right and follow the road for a short distance, reaching Cross House, where you can see the base of an ancient cross at the side of the house (on the 1840s OS map it is located at the road junction).

Take the track to the left of the house (Abbey Lane), and pass the caravan park and Abbey Farm. Immediately after Abbey Farm, turn right through a gate and walk along the side of a field - the remains of Burscough Priory can be seen in the garden on your right.

[If you are starting your day from the 'Bull & Dog' on the A59 Ormskirk to Burscough road: dice with death crossing over the main road and take the road (Abbey Lane) almost opposite the pub to the recycling centre (in a south-easterly direction). Pass the recycling centre and keep to the right of the industrial units and head for the railway; this path is muddy after rain. Take

care crossing the railway - it's only a single line but obviously trains can come from either direction. After a short distance, go through a small gate and immediately left through another small gate and walk along the edge of the field at the side of Abbey Farm and Abbey Cottage].

All these names are a bit of a give-away, for, if you look through the trees and undergrowth on your right, you can see the remains of Burscough Priory. It is possible to get a photo of the two piers from the public path during the winter months.

Cross House & base of wayside cross

Burscough Priory
OS Map Reference:
SD43408 09945

Access: none; on private land. View from
public footpath alongside Abbey Farm.

The Augustinian Priory at Burscough
was established by Robert of Lathom
around the year 1190, and was dedicated to St Nicholas; the canons followed
the Rule of St Augustine. Excavations
made in the nineteenth century uncovered the following parts of the priory as
well as the church: part of the cloister,
almonry, Beggars Yard, the Stanley family
Chantry in the North Transept, Chapter
House, monks' locutory, guest hall, and
guest locutory.

If these buildings, such as the beggars'
yard, almonry and guest hall, were used
for purpose, it would seem that the
priory took seriously its role of not only
praying for the souls of founders, but to
look after the needy and the traveller.

As well as this, the priory was responsi-
ble for a leper hospital, founded before
1200 at Ridgate (Rudgate, near Tarbock,
between Childwall and Widnes); according to Knowles it moved to Burscough
before 1311, but the site is unknown. At
the priory, two people received board
for life, and £7 per annum was given out
as alms to the poor.

Income for the priory came from
demesne lands in Burscough, Merton,
Ormskirk and Dalton, as well as the rectories of Ormskirk, Huyton, Radcliffe-
on-Soar (Nottinghamshire), Aughton,
North Meols, Sefton and Halsall.

All that remains above ground of
Burscough Priory are two massive

Map: 2-2

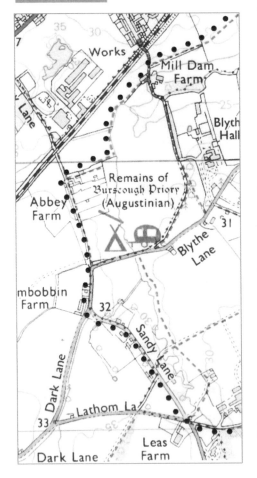

Lectern from Burscough Priory

had taken place 'at Burscough Abbey, which is now nearly demolished'.

A year earlier, on the opening of the Liverpool, Ormskirk and Preston Railway, the following description was given: 'The line of railway next traverses a spot once deemed sacred from all secular intrusion.

Within a stone's throw from the railway are the only two walls that now remain of the once famed structure of Burscough Priory'. Two marble effigies and the tenor bell, originally cast in 1497, were moved to Ormskirk Church; the bell is now on display at the east end of the north aisle.

piers, being the northeast and northwest piers of the central tower of the church, and foundations of the south transept and west end of the chancel; it is thought these remains are early Gothic, late thirteenth century.

A plan of the site was produced after the excavations mentioned above. At the Dissolution, the Earl of Derby attempted to save the church, as generations of his family were buried there, but to no avail. A newspaper report in 1850 mentions that 'within living memory' funerals

The massive squat tower of Ormskirk Church was built to house the bells from Burscough Priory. (For sources of information on the priory see Appendix 1 and Appendix 4).

Follow the path until you meet the Abbey Brook (previously Eller Brook on Yates' and OS 1840s maps), turn left and follow the path alongside the brook, cross over a footbridge and head for Mill Dam Farm. There is a way-marked path through the farm buildings; on reach-

Map: 2-3

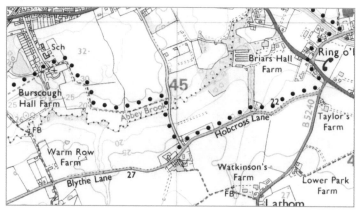

ing the track turn left for about 50 yards and take way-marked path on the right across a field. On reaching a wooded area, the way-marked path continues straight ahead across the next field; this is a field with a difference. You are warned that it is an old landfill site and there is a danger of explosions - so smokers, stub it out..........!
[2-3]

On reaching a track, cross over and go straight ahead over the next field until you reach a lane. Walk straight on and reach the end of a cul-de-sac, Chapel Lane, where you will see on the right the early seventeenth-century Burscough Hall Farmhouse and next to it the early nineteenth century Catholic Church of St John the Evangelist.

The path carries straight on and then right around the graveyard. Follow the path between the fields; as the path turns east, keep to the right of the drain.

Cross a footbridge and carry on alongside fields until reaching the road (Flax Lane). Turn right up to the junction with Blythe Lane/Hobcross Lane, and turn left. Walk to the junction with Hall Lane, go left to the roundabout on the main road, and left again. (Buses to Burscough/Ormskirk/Parbold on this main road). After about 150 yards, turn right towards the Leeds and Liverpool Canal and the Ring O Bells pub (still open!) on the canal-side and allow yourself a breather!

St John the Evangelist

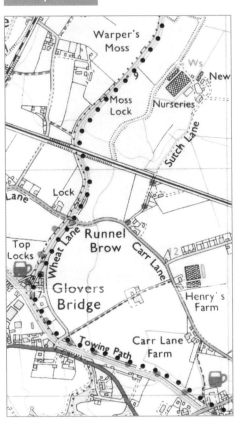

[2-4] Head west along the towpath, and join the Rufford Branch at Top Locks. Walk along the Branch of the Leeds-Liverpool canal up to Rufford. [Maps 2-5, 2-6] The Church of St Mary the Virgin (SD46420 15690) was built in 1869 on the site of a chapel built in 1736. That chapel was built on or near the site of an earlier chapel first mentioned in 1346 when it was endowed with a chantry.

It was suppressed in 1548 but refounded in 1553. Apparently it was again suppressed in the reign of Elizabeth. Its churchyard was still in use in the 17th century, where today you can see the base of a preaching cross dated 1000AD.
[Total miles to date = 19].

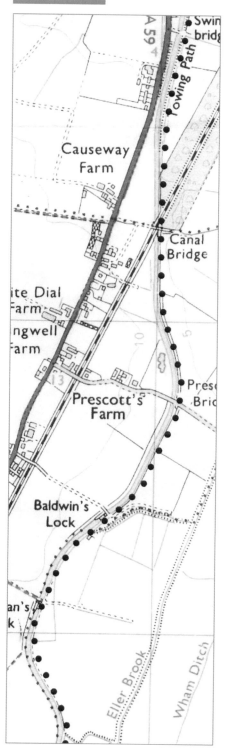

Top Locks, Rufford Branch

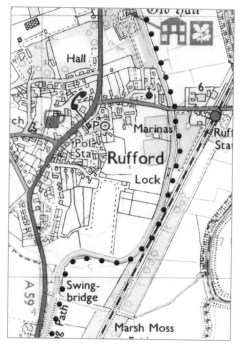

3 Rufford to the start of the Ribble Way at Longton
[7.5 miles]

Ordnance Survey map: **Explorer 285, 286**

Public transport: at Rufford, buses travel on the A59 to Ormskirk, Tarleton, etc, and also to Southport. Rufford train station is on the Ormskirk - Preston line. At the beginning of the Ribble Way, buses to Southport and Preston are available in Longton (1.5 mile walk along Marsh Lane).

[3-1] Starting from Rufford Church, follow the canal up to Sollom lock, passing Rufford Old Hall, the oldest part of which is the fascinating late fifteenth century hall. There is no path beyond Sollom lock, where the waterway follows the course of the original river Douglas.

[3-2] At the lock take the track to the right and immediately on the left cross a stile and keep to the right edge of the field. You eventually come to another stile on the right leading back onto the track. [3-3] Turn left up the track until reaching the river. Cross the stile on the left before crossing the river. Follow the path between the river and a cultivated field to the road bridge on the A59.

Rufford Old Hall

Make your way round the edge of the field and reach a gate and stile, from where you can walk to the road. [Alternative route from Sollom Lock: turn left up Lock Lane and at end of the lane turn right (see the base of possible medieval cross on the corner); just as you reach the A59 (immediately after the last house) turn right down a track alongside the house - there is no sign, but it is a public right of way. After a short while the track bends to the left, and then carries on along what can be a very muddy track to join the A59. Turn right and you pass St Mary's Church, which is on your right, and soon cross the canal and river]. A short distance to your left on the

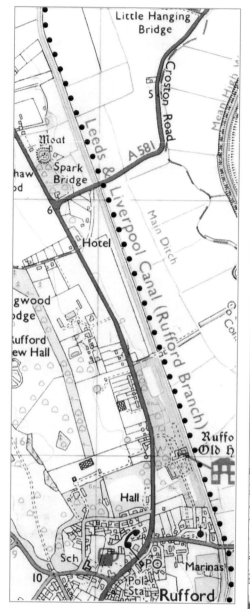

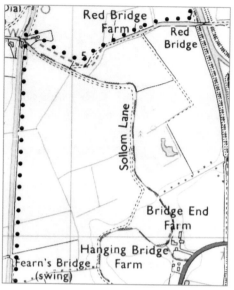

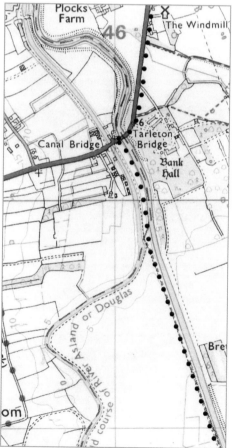

main road is the early eighteenth-century Church of St Mary.

Unfortunately the next part of the walk requires you to turn right and walk along the main road (there is a pavement), passing Bank Hall on your right, as you need to remain on the right hand side of the river and there is no alternative route. You may see a windmill, less its sails, on the right.

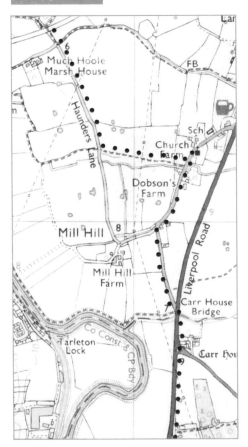

[3-4] On reaching the small road island, (where there was a toll house until a few years ago), you can get a glimpse of Carr House, famous as the place where Jeremiah Horrocks viewed the Transit of Venus in 1639; it is now a private house.

"Much Hoole was the centre of the astronomical universe in June 2004 when the first Transit of Venus (across the face of the sun) of the 21st century took place; and again on 5-6 June 2012!"

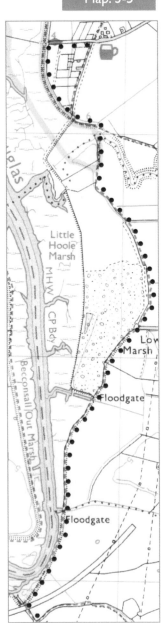

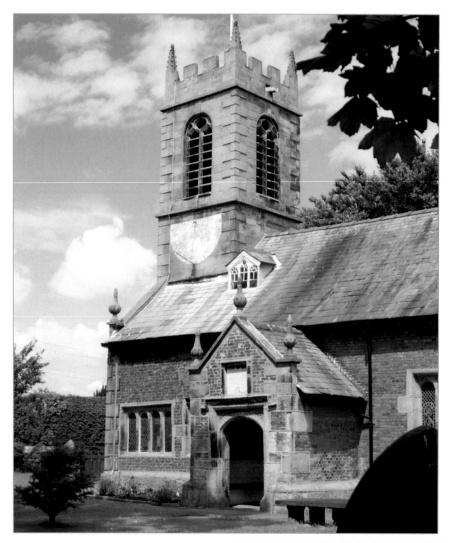

Carry on up the A59 a short distance and take the first lane on the left; eventually you reach St Michael's Church, where Horrocks was a curate.

Retrace your steps along the road for about 100 yards, to take the footpath on the right across a field to Haunders Lane. Turn right and head towards the river Douglas; there was an old railway just before river bank. [3-5]

Turn right along the river bank, pass two floodgates, until you reach the end of Station Road. Take the path opposite and

St Michael's Church, Much Hoole

carry on along the bank (On the OS map this path looks as though it's a dead end - but it isn't!). Cross two stiles, and after the second one follow the way-markers sharp left along the edge of a field to gain the raised river bank leading to the beginning of the Ribble Way.

A few hundred yards inland you will find the Dolphin Inn (SD 45892 25441), the official starting point of the Ribble Way. [Total miles to date = 26.5]

4 Start of the Ribble Way to Avenham Park, Preston

[7.5 miles]

Ordnance Survey map: **Explorer 286**

Public transport: for the beginning of the Ribble Way, buses to Southport and Preston are available in Longton (1.5 mile walk along Marsh Lane). In Preston there are ample trains and buses to many locations; from Avenham Park the station is a ten minute walk, and the bus station about 15 minutes..

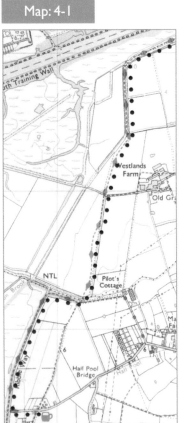

Map: 4-1

[4-1] Leave the Dolphin Inn and make your way to the raised river bank, over the stile and on your way to Penwortham. On the left are Longton and Hutton Marshes; on leaving the river Douglas you reach the Ribble after about two miles.

[4-2] After a further mile, on the far bank you can see the outlet of the Ribble Link/ Savick Brook, which was opened in 2002 to link the Lancaster Canal with the Ribble and thence the Douglas, the Rufford branch of the Leeds-Liverpool canal and the rest of the canal network.

[4-3] [4-4] After passing Penwortham golf course and just before the electricity sub-station, take the path to the right up the wooded hill, passing the club house and reach Clive Road. Turn left along Clive Road to reach the area of the former Penwortham Priory; turn left along Priory Lane, right down Priory Crescent, right

along Hollinhurst Ave (the priory site is on the right), and almost immediately left and left again to reach St Mary's Church.

This promontory also sported a motte and bailey castle, which seems to have lasted until around 1232 only.

Map: 4-2

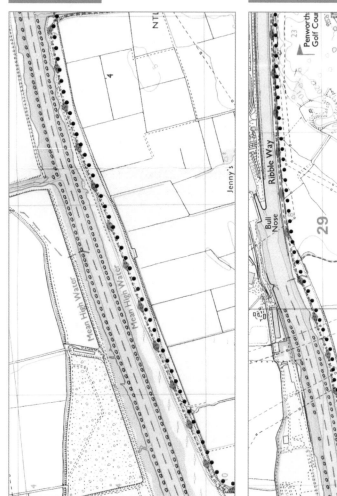

Map: 4-3

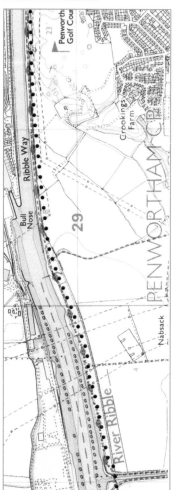

Map: 4-4

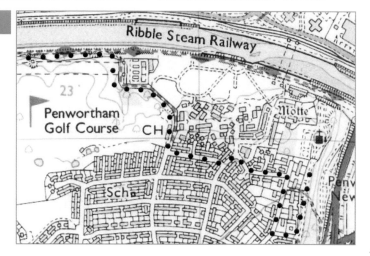

Penwortham Priory
OS Map Reference: SD 52240 28850
Access: there are no remains of the priory;
for services, news etc of the church of St
Mary phone 01772 743143 or see
http://www.penwortham-stmary.co.uk

There are, unfortunately, no remains of
the Benedictine priory at Penwortham,
the only surviving connection with the
priory being the parish church of St
Mary, which was served by three monks
and a chaplain from the priory.

The priory was on a raised site with
extensive views of the valley down
which the Ribble flowed, described then
as a noble river, abounding in salmon.
Dedicated to St Mary, the priory was
established in the first half of the twelfth
century (the date is disputed) by Warin
Bussel, baron of Penwortham, and the
Abbot of Evesham Abbey in Worcester-
shire, as a cell of that abbey; the priory
never became independent of Evesham.

As well as St Mary's church, other gifts
to the abbey included land in Penwortham, Longton, Howick, Farington,
part of Great Marton, pensions from the
churches of Leyland and North Meols,
and a share of fishing rights in the Ribble.

A breviary which was used by the
monks in St Mary's Church is held in the
British Library; it was written and illustrated around 1300 - 1319 and presented to the parish church of Penwortham
in 1486; it 'is one of the most complete
examples of the text and music of the
Divine Office according to Sarum Use'.
(BL Manuscripts Catalogue).

Little is known of most of the priors,
except the good Prior Wicote who

St Mary's Church

looked after his monks, and the scan-
dalous Prior Norris, formerly abbot of
Evesham but banished to Penwortham.

By the sixteenth century there were
only two or three monks remaining,
finally leaving the priory around 1535,
after which it was leased to John Fleetwood of London. The priory was used
as a dwelling, but much altered, and in
1832 was replaced by a new building
(also called Penwortham Priory), which
was demolished in the 1920s.

The site is now under a housing estate.
There is the pedestal of a wayside cross
on the avenue leading to St Mary's
Church, the cross itself being modern.
We can presume that, though small, the
priory had a library, as the cartulary
states that

'a monastery without a library was like a castle without an armoury'.

Most monasteries would have a library, with sources to aid the monks' studying and liturgical day, including service and scriptural books, devotional reading and text books.

The priory did not neglect the needy, as twenty shillings a year were given to the leper hospital on the far bank of the Ribble in Preston (it ceased to operate as a hospital around 1465, but the chapel remained), and £7-13-4d was given to the poor at Penwortham and Leyland. Today, very near the site of the former priory, there is the Priory Park Care Centre - providing care for elderly people! The priory's net income in 1535 was £29-18-7d.
(For sources of information on the priory see Appendix 1 and Appendix 5).

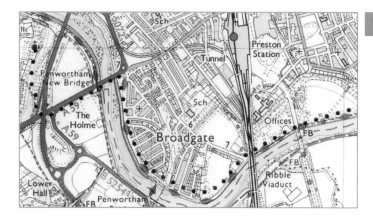

Map: 4-5

[4-5] On leaving St Mary's Church, make your way down to the river and cross over the road bridge, turning right along the river path along Broadgate. Soon you reach the old Penwortham Bridge. Carry on along Riverside, under the railway bridge and into Miller Park, then into Avenham Park (SD 53920 28729) (http://www.preston.gov.uk/yourservices/culture-parks-and-events/avenham-and-miller-parks/).

This is a very quiet and pleasant walk, and you can be quite oblivious of the fact that beyond the trees there is a city of over 130,000 souls! Avenham Park boasts a new Pavilion, opened officially in 2009, which includes a welcome cafe. From here you can visit the sites of St Mary Magdalen's Hospital, Preston Friary and Tulketh Abbey

- there are, however, no visible remains of any of them.

"... you can be quite oblivious of the fact that beyond the trees there is a city of over 130,000 souls!"

[Total miles to date = 34].

Preston Friars
OS Map Reference: SD 53400 29460

The Friars Minor (Grey Friars) of the Blessed Virgin Mary, were established in what is now Marsh Lane in Preston around 1260, possibly by Edmund, Earl of Lancaster, younger son of Henry III. Leland mentions the site as belonging to the Preston family, of which several members were buried there; in excavations in 2006, several graves were uncovered (report not yet published).

Leland also states that Sir Robert de Holland was buried there; he had established the priory at Upholland. The friars were different from monastic orders as they spent their time outside their friary within the local community, preaching and doing missionary work, so their houses were usually located in towns.

The friary buildings were described as including a small quadrangle with cloister and chapel; the shell of the chapel was still in existence at the beginning of the nineteenth century. At its dissolution in 1539 it was sold, along with the friaries of Lancaster and Warrington, to Thomas Holcroft for £126-10-0.

"... the friary became a House of Correction, until 1789."

Some time later, (probably in the first half of the seventeenth century - the friary is still shown on a Lancashire Record Office map prior to 1642), the friary became a House of Correction, until 1789.

(For sources of information on the Friary, see Appendix 1 and Appendix 6).

Tulketh Abbey
OS Map Reference: SD 52240 30150

Tulketh Abbey must be one of the most short-lived monastic foundations in the country, being established on 4th July 1124 and then moved to Furness in 1127. It was established by Stephen Count of Boulogne and later King of England. It was located in the grounds of Tulketh Hall; the site is now covered with houses.

It was a Cistercian abbey, the first Savigniac house founded in England. The ruins are mentioned in West's 'Antiquities of Furness' in 1774:

'On a rising ground, at a small distance to the south west of Tulket Hall, some ruins, and part of the fosse (moat) which surrounded the principal buildings of that monastery, are still visible'.

However, West believed that the monks used existing buildings, possibly Roman, for their abbey, rather than constructing new buildings.

(For sources of information on the abbey, see Appendix 1 and Appendix 7).

Preston Hospital
OS Map Reference: SD 52980 29890

St Mary Magdalen's hospital for lepers was in existence by 1177, probably under the patronage of the lords of the Honour of Lancaster. It was situated very close to the present church of St Walburge - a stone coffin and other remains have been found when local building work has taken place, e.g. St Walburge's, the cutting for the railway, and the Maudland estate.

"The chapel was evidently a place of pilgrimage"

The hospital was disused by 1465, and its chapel (in disrepair) was dissolved in 1548, the land eventually being bought by Thomas Fleetwood of Penwortham. A copy of the seal of the hospital is held in the Harris Museum in Preston. The chapel was evidently a place of pilgrimage, as in 1355 the Pope gave a relaxation of penance to those who visited the chapel on the principal feasts of the year and those of St Mary Magdalen and St Thomas of Canterbury. Penwortham Priory gave twenty shillings a year to the hospital.

(For sources of information on the Hospital, see Appendix 1 and Appendix 8.)

5 Avenham Park, Preston to Ladyewell Shrine, Fernyhalgh

[8.5 miles]

Ordnance Survey map: **Explorer 286**

Public transport: in Preston there are ample trains and buses to many locations; to Avenham Park from the train station is a ten minute walk, and from the bus station about 15 minutes. At Ladyewell, for the nearest buses, either return down the road you came, under the motorway and continue to Longsands Lane to take a bus to Preston town centre (about 0.75 mile walk); or take the footpath opposite Ladyewell House, follow the path which takes you over the M6, turn right then left onto Pittman Way (about 0.5 mile walk).

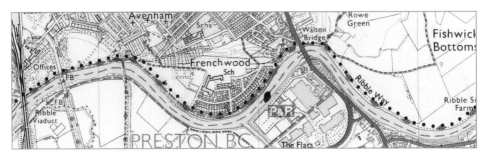

Map: 5-1

[5-1] This section begins in Avenham Park. Walk along the lovely tree-lined path by the river and as you reach the end of Avenham Park look for the Tram Bridge over the river - the builders of the Lancaster Canal never built a canal crossing for boats over the river Ribble, so goods had to be unloaded, taken over the tram bridge and reloaded on the other side of the river. The path continues alongside the river (the River Darwen enters the river Ribble on the far side) and eventually reaches London Road/Walton Bridge.

Cross over the road (not the bridge) and walk down beside the Shaw's Arms pub, taking the path alongside the river once more. (Handy bench here!). As the path divides, look for a stile on your right, taking you alongside the river; the stile has a Ribble Way sign, sometimes covered by

undergrowth. (If you carry on along the track, you are going the wrong way!).

[5-2] On the high ground over the river you see St Leonard's Church. Carry on along the side of the river with Fishwick Bottoms on left, pass Mellings Wood and walk under the motorway. [5-3]

After the motorway the path moves away from the river briefly and rises onto Red Scar, with the river many feet below and out of sight. On the left you see the crematorium and just beyond a public footpath [SD 58640 32259] which takes you back to the road if you need to break your journey here. [Buses back to Preston from here].

You may wish to visit the Ladyewell Shrine in Fernyhalgh from this point. Take the

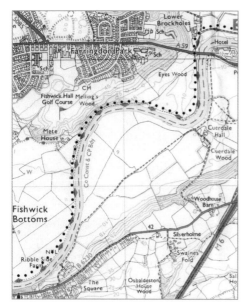

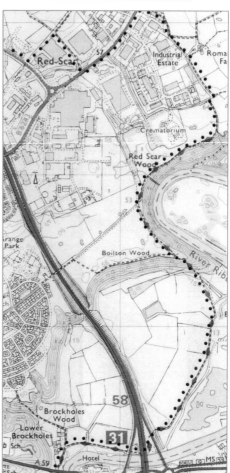

path from the Ribble Way to the Preston-Longridge road, turn left along the road for about 500 yards, cross the road and take the public footpath close to the bus stop. [5-4]

After about 300 yards you reach the site of the old Preston-Longridge railway; turn left along the tarmaced path of the old railway and on reaching the road, turn right and make for the traffic island. There are no public footpath signs here, but take the right turn at the island and immediately

Map: 5-4

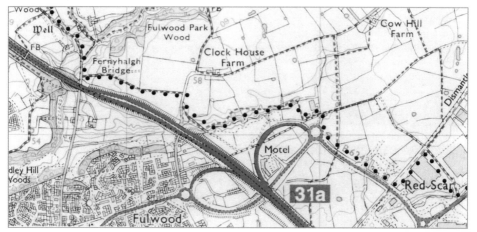

look for a farm on the left (Little Rough Hey Farm).

Turn left in front of the farmhouse and cross a stile ahead (ignore the barking dog - it's on a long chain!). Follow the path through another gate, then walk parallel with the motorway slip-road.

After passing the field on the right, take the right hand path down towards the stream; carry along beside the stream, over a footbridge, and eventually reach a track. Turn right, walk down and round two hair-pin bends, cross the stream and walk uphill, reaching a road.

A few yards after the 'private road' sign, find a path on the left. Cross over two fields, and take a short track down to the road; turn right, crossing Savick Brook. Take the footpath directly ahead (to the right of The Mount driveway), and walk up through the trees on what is reputed to be a very old pilgrim track.

On reaching the gate at the top you find the Ladyewell Shrine immediately on the right. Half a mile further up the road is St Mary's Church.
[Total miles to date = 42.5].

Ladyewell Shrine, Fernyhalgh
OS Map Reference: SD 55616 33627

Our Lady's Well at Fernyhalgh is a place of pilgrimage to this day. This once quiet and isolated shrine, has still a peaceful atmosphere, even with the background music of Britain's first motorway.

"... one gets a true feeling of a pilgrim way, as for centuries people have walked this way to reach the Well."

Walking up the wooded gully down which the water from the Well descends one gets a true feeling of a pilgrim way, as for centuries people have walked this way to reach the Well. The present Ladyewell House incorporates a chapel built in 1685 and used until St Mary's Church was built half a mile up Fernyhalgh Lane in 1793/4.

There is evidence of earlier chapels on the Ladyewell House site, one being in existence before 1348-9; the chapel existing at the Dissolution was destroyed. The house seems to have been used for Mass and services even during Penal times. Besides the house and well, the site has an ancient cross, with a possibly restored head.
(For sources of information on Ladyewell, see Appendix 1 and Appendix 9).

6 Ladyewell Shrine, Fernyhalgh to Ribchester

[8.5 miles]

Ordnance Survey map: **Explorer 286, 287**

Public transport: at Ladyewell, for the nearest buses, either return down the road you came, under the motorway and continue to Longsands Lane to take a bus to Preston town centre (about 0.75 mile walk); or take the footpath opposite Ladyewell House, follow the path which takes you over the M6, turn right then left onto Pittman Way (about 0.5 mile walk). At Ribchester, there are buses to Longridge, Clitheroe, Blackburn etc..

St Mary's Church, Fernyhalgh

Starting from the Ladyewell Shrine, return to the Ribble Way by the same route; from here to Ribchester follow the Ribble Way.

[6-1] As you reach the Ribble Way, don't cross over the stile but go left along the edge of the field, and the next field; the path then descends sharply into a ravine, over a footbridge and up the far side. When you emerge from the wood, walk diagonally right across the field where you meet a road; turn left along the road. Carry on along the road, which bears left (with Big Wood on your right), then turns right then left. After crossing what was a Roman road (no longer visible), the road takes a sharp right turn.

[6-2] Just after Marsh House, take the path on the left, crossing two fields and head for the left-hand corner of the second field, leading you on to Alston Lane, with Alston Hall down the lane on the right. Cross the lane, head straight over the field and down into a dip, up the far side and across the field, where for a short while you walk along a path which once was a Roman road.

"... walk along a path which once was a Roman road."

[6-3] On reaching the modern road, turn right, pass Hothersall Lodge and Hothersall Hall (http://www.hothersallhall.org/index.htm), then up the field ahead; at this stage you are close to, but above, the Ribble. Pass the Boat House and Lower Barn Farm, and you soon see St Wilfrid's Church in Ribchester (SD 64996 35025) on the left.

On reaching the river, walk along the riverside and into the village of Ribchester. Ribchester Roman Museum can be found on the lane leading up to the Church. [Total miles to date = 51]

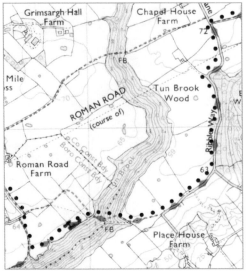

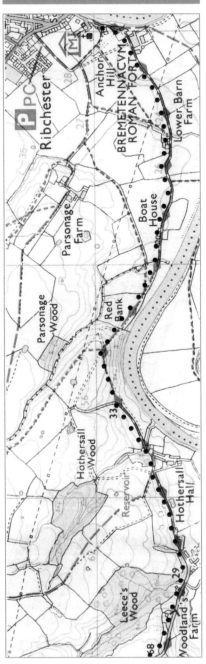

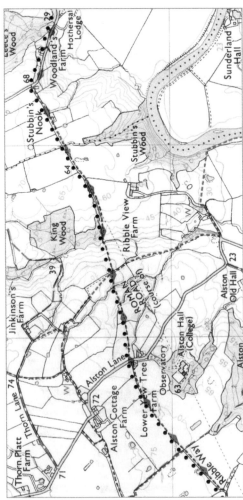

7 Ribchester to Whalley Abbey via Stydd

[8.5 miles]

Ordnance Survey map: **Explorer 286, 287**

Public transport: at Ribchester, there are buses from Longridge, Clitheroe, Blackburn etc. At Whalley, there are buses to Clitheroe, Preston, Blackburn, etc; and also rail link to Clitheroe and Blackburn.

Stydd Hospital and St Saviour's Chapel
OS Map Reference: SD 65389 35968 **Access:** open during the day.
For services, etc phone 01254 878352.

This lovely chapel has a really medieval atmosphere about it, giving the impression that not much has changed over its more than 800 year history.

The hospital, with chapel, of St Saviour was founded by Richard de Singleton and later given to the Knights Hospitallers, whose aim originally was to provide pilgrims to the Holy Land with hospices (accommodation for pilgrims or travellers) and hospitals.

The hospital, sometimes called the hospital at Langrigh (Longridge), ceased to function by the early fourteenth century, but the chapel remains; there is nothing of the hospital itself to be

seen today. Around 1853 the chapel was in use once a month, and today is still used once a month for Evening Prayer during the summer months. Excavations have found possible Roman remains on the site, not surprising as it is so close to the important Roman crossroads of Ribchester. George Latham's sketches of the chapel around 1853 show foliage growing out of the walls, windows and roof; and inside is a screen and benches - the latter have now been replaced by chairs, the design of which reflects the design of the Gothic chancel window.

(For sources of information on St Saviour's Chapel, see Appendix 1 and Appendix 10).

[7-1] After visiting St Wilfrid's Church and the Roman Museum in Ribchester, walk along the river path around the village, onto the main road and turn right, pass the Ribchester Arms and take the first left along Stydd Lane. The Catholic Church of St Peter and St Paul and almshouses are on your left; keep straight ahead across a field to a little gem - St Saviour's Chapel.

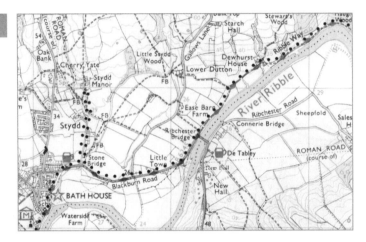

Map: 7-1

Return to the main road and turn left. This stretch of busy road, with a very narrow footpath, is part of a Roman Road from Ribchester to Elslack. On reaching the road bridge, don't cross the river but carry straight ahead along the north side of river. On reaching Dewhurst House Farm, look for a path down to the riverside just before the farm buildings. This path can be quite muddy. [7-2]

The path follows the riverside until the river loops south, when the path cuts across through woods and turns north, across two fields, behind Hey Hurst and then east again. Just before Trough House, look for a path to the right towards the footbridge over the Ribble. [7-3]

Cross the river and take the path left towards Dinckley Hall (private). Just before Dinckley Hall, turn right along a tarmaced lane which leads through Dinckley Wood. Follow this quiet road, pass The Nook on the left and after a double bend in the road, take the road on the left, Moorgate Lane; after a double bend the road follows

the course of the Roman road mentioned above. Where the road bends to the left at Aspinall's Farm, go straight ahead through the farm.

On reaching a large field, walk diagonally right across the field in an east-south-east direction down to a footbridge over Dinckley Brook; carry on up the far side and aim for a small group of buildings (including the Black Bull Inn) on the main road (Old Langho Road).

[7-4] Turn left along the main road. [Alternative route: from Dinckley Hall: shortly after the lane straightens out, look for a path on the left. This path arches round the first field; cross over a stile (way-marked Ribchester Walks) and turn right keeping alongside the hedge, to another way-marked stile; cross and keep right, along two sides of the field, cross a further small field to a track, with Craven Fold Farm on your left.

The way-marker on the stile points right, but look left near the farm and follow the

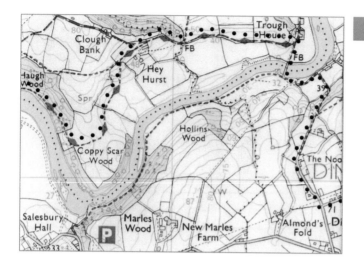

Map: 7-2

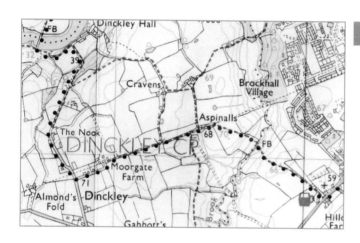

Map: 7-3

Map: 7-4

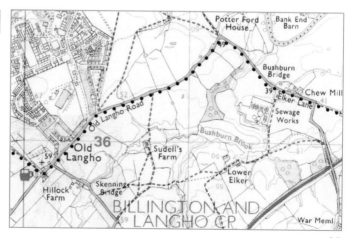

way-marked path behind the farm buildings. The path leads down to a footbridge over Dinckley Brook and up to a road leading down to Blackburn Rovers training ground. Cross the road and walk along the straight track immediately south of the training ground.

Stay on the track until it ceases, and cross the field ahead, immediately north of Brockhall Village; cross the stile and turn right along a farm track for a short distance, then bear left towards Hacking Wood; walk along the edge of the wood, where the track eventually reaches the road; go straight down the road in a south-easterly direction].

The road isn't too busy but has no footpath. At the first 90 degree bend to the right, stay on the main road. [7-5] Where the road bends sharp right again (SD 71780 36241), carry straight ahead along a footpath from where you can see Whalley Viaduct ahead. Take care crossing the very busy A59; once over the road, go immediately left (with a fence on your right) for a few yards, then go right to cross a field. There is a stile into a small triangular field; keep along the left-hand hedge, through a gate and onto a road; go left along Dale View, right along Sunnyside Ave and find the path alongside the viaduct.

Cross the footbridge over the river Calder and turn first right and pass under the abbey's massive west gatehouse. The entrance to Whalley Abbey is along this road, on the right.

[Total miles to date = 59.5]

Map: 7-5

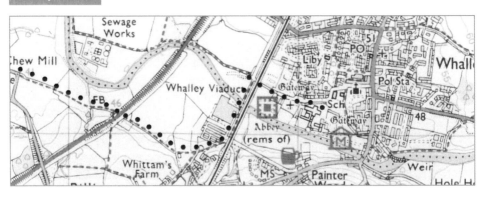

8 Whalley Abbey to Sawley Abbey
[10 miles]

Ordnance Survey map: **Explorer 287, OL41**
Public transport: at Whalley, there are buses from Clitheroe, Preston, Blackburn, etc; and also a rail link from Clitheroe and Blackburn. At Sawley, there are buses to Preston, Clitheroe, Barnoldswick, Skipton,etc..

Whalley Abbey
OS Map Reference: SD 73093 36088
Access: open to the public daily; see www.whalleyabbey.co.uk/ for full details.

and in Rochdale. The churches of Eccles, Rochdale, Blackburn and Whalley were appropriated to the abbey, which also had other granges including those at Staining and Marland (Rochdale), as well as at Stanlaw.

Set in a beautiful valley with the river Calder flowing alongside, the abbey and church was for over 200 years a place of pilgrimage and a place where the poor and needy could find some relief. According to the Valor Ecclesiasticus prior to the Dissolution, the abbey set aside over £116 (c £50,000 today) for alms-giving and support of the poor, which included keeping 24 'poor and feeble folk', and helping the casual poor turning up at the monastery.

After over a hundred years at Stanlaw at Ellesmere Port in Cheshire, the congregation of Cistercian monks moved to Whalley where the new abbey, 'Locus Benedictus de Whalley', of St Mary the Virgin was established on 4 April 1296 by Henry de Lacy, 3rd Earl of Lincoln.

The site at Stanlaw remained as a grange of Whalley Abbey until the Dissolution. As can be gauged from today's extensive remains, Whalley Abbey was of a considerable size, built to accommodate up to 60 monks, although this number was probably never achieved.

Over the years its holdings were extensive, including land in Whalley, Billington, part of Wiswell, part of Read

The abbot's lodging and infirmary have, surprisingly, survived to this day and are still in use. Also still surviving are the two massive gatehouses. along with extensive remains of the rest of the complex. The stalls from the abbey were relocated to the parish church, and 13 icons are currently in Blackburn Art Gallery. There are 18th and 19th century illustrations of the remains by

Nathaniel Buck, William Latham and John Weld.

The income of the abbey before the Dissolution was just over £321; in 1534 there were 21 monks in residence.

The abbey was dissolved in 1537 and the last abbot, Abbot Paslew, was executed along with two monks for their involvement in the Pilgrimage of Grace. The abbey is now owned by the Church of England Diocese of Blackburn, with a

Mission Statement: 'To continue to be a holy place that draws and points people to God and offers them an experience of peace'.

In St Mary's churchyard nearby, there are three 9th - 11th century high crosses. Knowles believes there may have been a much earlier monastic foundation in Whalley. (For sources of information on Whalley Abbey, see Appendix 1 and Appendix 11).

[8-1] From Whalley Abbey, return along 'The Sands', under the west gateway and under the railway viaduct. Carry on along the track straight ahead which eventually leads underneath the A59. A few yards further on look for a worn path across a field to the right (not way-marked); this path crosses a small brook - keep to the left-hand side on the next two fields then cut across where the field rises to a junction of paths.

Map: 8-1

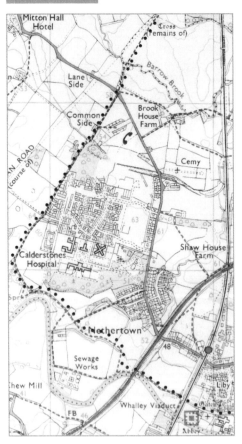

Follow the path straight ahead way-marked Mitton. After the next gate, turn right along a track which takes you round Calderstones Hospital. Cross over the road (B6246), taking the path ahead through the woods. Cross Barrow Brook and walk straight ahead, where the path follows the course of a very ancient way - a Roman road from Ribchester to Skipton.

[8-2] Soon you reach the base of a wayside cross, its presence indicating that this was a well-used route in the middle ages and anyone travelling from Whalley Abbey to Sawley Abbey would have used this most direct route.

However, today not much of the route of the Roman road is accessible, so leave the path at the cross base and go left towards the fence and go through a small gate, up a gully and across fields, with views of Great

St Nicholas' Hospital (sometimes called Edisford Hospital) for lepers was situated away from the town of Clitheroe, as was normal to avoid infection, in the fields by the river in what is now the Edisford/Low Moor area.

It was founded before 1211, but it is not known when it ceased to be a leper hospital; there were no lepers there in 1386-7. It remained as a chantry until the Reformation. A cartulary exists for 1317 in the Lancashire Record Office (Ref: DDTO: Edisford leper hospital cartulary 1317).
(For sources of information on Clitheroe Hospital, see Appendix 1).

Mitton Church on the left. Go through Shuttleworth Farm and out onto the road; turn right along the road - you are now back on the Ribble Way. [8-3]

Follow the road for about 0.75 miles and look for a path on the left just after crossing over Pendleton Brook. After about 50 yards go right at the junction over the stile and follow the path back to the Ribble's edge. Follow the path along the river, with Siddows Hall on the right, pass a caravan park to Edisford Bridge, where there are toilets and picnic area and an ice-cream van if you are lucky!

There are various routes into Clitheroe if you wish to visit this interesting town. Continuing the walk, go up the road away from the bridge and walk left by the swimming pool. [8-4]

Follow the path through Low Moor (don't be tempted to turn left - they're all dead-ends) and walk to the weir, with Waddow Hall (http://www.waddow.org.uk/home.aspx) on the opposite bank. (There is a path to the right into Clitheroe town, if needed).

[Alternative route: If you are starting from Clitheroe town centre, leave along King Street (perhaps armed with home-made apple pie from delicatessen and sweets from the traditional sweet shop Chocolate Box in King Street!) towards the station,

turn right then left under the railway bridge and along Kirkmoor Road; turn right (also called Kirkmoor Road) and as the road bends to the left, take the footpath on the right across a field.

Cross two more fields heading more or less straight ahead - look back to get an unusual view of Clitheroe Castle. At the next field, follow the path diagonally across the field to the river. Turn right along the river; there may be diversions from the river path from time to time].

At Brungerley Bridge, turn right up Waddington Road for around 50 yards then left (surprisingly, there are public toilets let into the hillside here!). It's a pleasant walk through trees, with views from a higher path, with benches, if you need a break.

"...West Bradford, where Gandhi spent a few days on his visit to Lancashire in September 1931."

As the river bends to the right, you reach the abandoned Cross Hill Quarry which is now a nature reserve. Near Bradford Bridge is the village of West Bradford, where Gandhi spent a few days on his visit to Lancashire in September 1931. On the right is the unmistakeable sight of Castle Cement works! [8-5]

As the river loops to the right, the path carries on through woods to the road north of Chatburn. The path on this road has been improved recently; follow the signs which take you across the road and left down the edge of a field, avoiding a bending dangerous stretch of road down to the river.

Cross over a side road and take the path indicated alongside the river for about 400 yards and cross over a bridge. Here the path turns directly right back along the other side of the river. [However, at times this stretch is closed, requiring a diversion through Grindleton; follow the path behind the church to meet the Ribble Way again at SD 76856 45618.

Grindleton Church is dedicated to St Ambrose of Milan, patron saint of beekeepers. The present church was built in 1805, with the foundation stone of a earlier chapel being built into the gateway]. If the path is not closed, follow the regular path along the north bank of the river. [8-6]

Just after Smithies Brook joins the Ribble, the path moves away from the river, across fields to the Sawley Road. Turn right along the road and down the hill; there is a short stretch of bankside footpath up to Sawley Bridge. Cross the bridge, turn right at the Spread Eagle Hotel, and Sawley Abbey is on the left. There are several listed buildings in Sawley village.

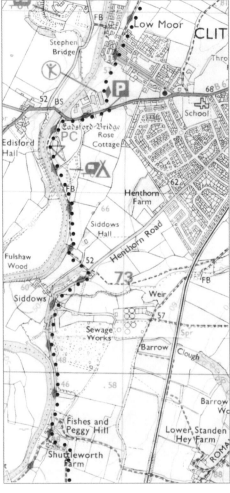

Map: 8-2
(far left)
Map: 8-3
(left)

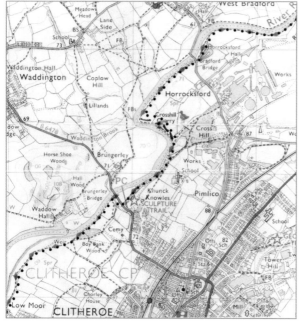

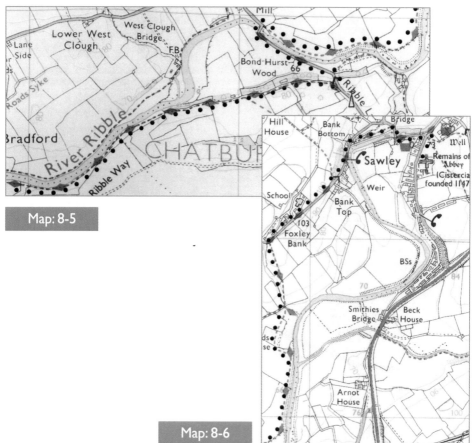

Sawley Abbey
OS Map Reference: SD 77698 46441
Access: the site is freely open to the public during the day; contact phone number is 0870 333 1181 or see www.english-heritage.org.uk.

Situated in the quiet of the Lancashire countryside, close to the river Ribble and with Pendle Hill in the background, is the peaceful abbey of St Mary and St Andrew at Sawley; in medieval times this area was part of Yorkshire. The remains on the ground are extensive, but not to any great height, apart from some of the mid-twelfth century abbey church.

This Cistercian abbey was established in 1147 by William de Percy when the abbot Benedict, with twelve monks and ten conversi, came down from Northumberland. Conversi, or lay brothers, were employed in the harder manual work of the house; this group of brothers later died out in monastic houses as working practices changed and the Black Death decimated the population. A record from 1481 shows there were about 30 monks and about 40 servants, but no lay brothers by that time.

There was some doubt as to whether the monks would stay at Sawley, as the land wasn't very productive, but the ab-

bey was saved from relocating by Maud, the daughter of the founder, who gave the monks the church of St Mary of Tadcaster, and an annual pension from the chapel of Newton. At the Dissolution there were 21 monks and 37 servants at the abbey. Because of his involvement with the Pilgrimage of Grace, the last abbot, Thomas Bolton, was executed in 1537. The 'Sawley Ballad', adopted as a marching song during the Pilgrimage of Grace, was probably written by a monk from Sawley.

"... the last abbot, Thomas Bolton, was executed in 1537."

It is thought that some parts of the abbey were moved and have been preserved: the Rood Screen to All Hallows Church, Great Mitton; a bay window to Little Mearley Hall; part of an archway to St Mary the Virgin Church, Gisburn; and a doorway to Wigglesworth Hall, North Yorkshire.

In the grounds of Downham Hall there are fragments of medieval masonry, possibly from Sawley Abbey, and three of the bells in Downham Church are said to have come from Sawley or Whalley Abbey. (For sources of information on Sawley Abbey, see Appendix 1 and Appendix 12).

[Total miles for Section One = **69.5**]

Cockerham Priory to Furness Abbey

9 Cockerham to Lancaster Canal at Aldcliffe
[9.5 miles]

Ordnance Survey map: **Explorer 296, OL41**

Public transport: there are buses to Cockerham from Lancaster and Knott End.
A short walk from the canal at Aldcliffe towards Lancaster brings you to the A6
road, where several buses operate. Lancaster also has a train station
on the main west coast line.

Cockerham Priory
OS Map Reference: SD46245 52174 ?

The manor of Cockerham was granted to Leicester Abbey in the mid-twelfth century, and by 1207 the abbot of Leicester had sent several Augustinian canons to establish a small priory, initially serving the parish church of St Michael.

St Michael's Church, Cockerham

It is not known where the priory was situated, but for practical reasons of access it is likely to have been near the church. The most likely place is what is now Cockerham Hall, on the other side of Marsh Lane from the church; the pre-

sent owner believes this to be the case. In 1400, by which time the canons had been withdrawn and a vicar appointed to the church, there was in the manor a hall with provision rooms, kitchens, brewhouse, barn, granary, stables, byres, a dovecote, orchard and courtyard, with several acres of land, with watermill and windmill; these may have developed from the priory.

> **"Rent was also obtained from making salt as there were twenty nine 'saltcotes' along the coast."**

Rent was also obtained from making salt, as there were twenty nine 'saltcotes' (huts containing apparatus for evaporating and preparing salt) along the coast. The priory, dissolved finally in 1477, was never independent, being a cell of Leicester Abbey. Some records were destroyed in a fire at the manor prior to 1477.

(For sources of information on Cockerham Priory, see Appendix 1 and Appendix 13).

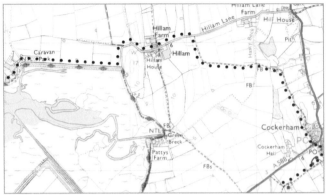

[9-1] This section of the walk begins at St Michael's Church, Cockerham, which is largely rebuilt but boasts a tower built towards the end of the 16th century.

Make your way from the church to the road, turn left and reach the A588. Turn left for a few yards, cross the road and take the lane ahead between houses (unmarked, but a public footpath). Note the high-chimneyed house on right - a former vicarage.

Carry on up the lane to pass Mill Hill cottage and straight ahead through what looks like their back garden, to find a rickety stile. Cross the fields ahead using the stiles; walk a short way along a track to Ware Cottage, but look for a stile on the right before the cottage; the route is via stiles and fields/gardens behind the cottage - its garden sporting a superior tree-house!

Walk diagonally across the field to a footbridge, then walk along the edge of the next field. Eventually the track goes through a gate and veers right towards the road; at the road, turn left and follow the road until it reaches the flood defence bank (probably covered in sheep with no road sense!) and the Lancashire Coastal Path; turn right along the road/bank towards Bank End. [9-2]

You can now follow the Lancashire Coastal Path up to the outskirts of Lancaster. The

path hugs the coast and soon veers north and you reach the higher ground where you find the remains of Cockersand Abbey. According to the information board on the remains of the Chapter House, in the

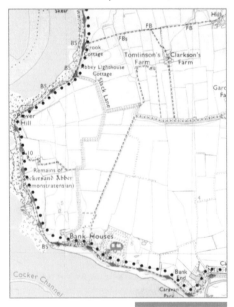

12th century the abbey was virtually an island during the winter floods, and surrounded by undrained marshland.

Cockersand Abbey
OS Map Reference: SD 42702 53760

Access: free access to the ruins, from the Lancashire Coastal Path.

The order of Premonstratensian Canons was founded in 1120 by St Norbert at Premontre in France, and followed the Rule of St Augustine.

'The monks ... of Cockersand must have been a hardy group of people,'

The monks of the Premonstratensian abbey of Cockersand must have been a hardy group of people, as the abbey was situated by the sea shore, with the prevailing winds, freezing cold in winter, whistling off the sea and finding every nook and cranny of the substantial abbey buildings; Leland describes it as being located.:

"on a very exposed site at the mercy of all the winds..."

A hermitage was established here about 1180, followed by a hospital a few years later, with the abbey of St Mary being founded around 1192 by William de Lancaster II; the hospital continued as part of the abbey until the Suppression - in 1536 there were 15 poor men maintained in the hospital.

The abbey held property and land in Preston Patrick (Cumbria), Warburton and Thurnham, as well as other gifts of land and rents, and also held the rectories of Garstang and Great Mitton. A grange existed at Pilling which, according to Marshall, acted as the abbey's home farm. The site of St John's Chapel (SD 4164 4857) is shown on the first edition 1:10000 map for 1840's, south-west of Pilling Hall.

The remains of Cockersand Abbey above ground today include the Chapter House and parts of the nave walls, and north and south transepts of the abbey church. The thirteenth century octagonal Chapter House was later used as a mausoleum for the Dalton family, so is still in reasonably good condition.

There must have been substantial parts of the buildings remaining in 1857 when Martin and Thomas Moran and Thomas McGowan were charged with stealing 200 pounds of lead from the abbey; for their pains they spent one year in the House of Correction at Lancaster. There are illustrations of the abbey as it was by John Weld (1830s) and Nathaniel Buck (1727-8).

It is reputed that two doorways and a double window from the abbey are built into a building at the nearby Crook Farm; and that the choir stalls were moved to Lancaster Priory Church, but this is by no means certain, as Tracy argues that Lancaster Priory itself would have been quite able to pay to have those Decorated choir stalls made for its own priory.

Cockersand Abbey was dissolved on 29 January 1539, with a value of £282; at that time there was an abbot and 22 canons, and 57 servants. The hospital at the abbey was dissolved at the same time. (For sources of information on Cockersand Abbey, see Appendix 1 and Appendix 14).

Map: 9-3

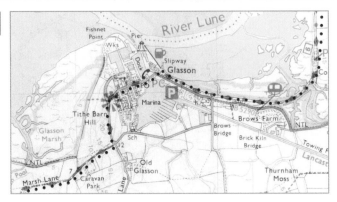

[9-3] From Cockersand Abbey, follow the coastal path north; the aim is to reach the Lancaster Canal, and there are various routes available: across the fields in an easterly direction from Crook Cottage to reach Ellel Hall Bridge; up to Glasson and follow the canal towpath, cut across to Ellel Hall Bridge from Bailey Bridge; and the preferred route here - along the Coastal Path and join the canal at Aldcliffe.

Turn right into a field at the south side of Crook Farm - hedgerows abound with blackberries in season! Follow the way-marked route, over Janson Pool and across a field to a line of ancient trees; turn right and walk alongside the trees to a gate. Go through another gate on the left of the caravan park and follow the track up to a crossroads and turn left.

At the next junction turn right and walk

down into Glasson; cross the bridge over the dock lock and head for the estuary footpath. From here to Aldcliffe you are walking on an old railway route from Lancaster to Glasson; the railway closed in 1964. [After a short while, notice a sign to

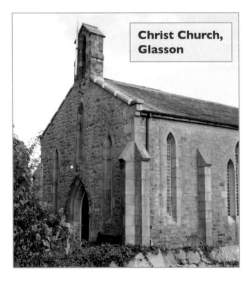

Christ Church, Glasson

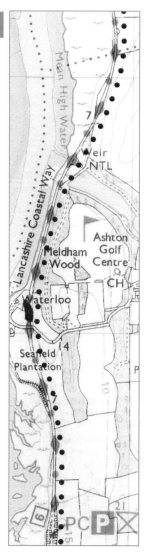

summer, anyway); you can see a little of the golf course, but not Ashton Hall, now the golf club house (their website gives some history of the Hall - www.lancastergc. co.uk/pages.php/index.html).

'a bit claustrophobic in autumn, but better in spring'

[9-5] About half a mile after the electricity pylons, take the footpath on the right towards Aldcliffe. Go straight across the first field, then left, hugging the hedge as it gradually turns east. On the left see a way-marked stile, and walk some distance on this narrow, hedge-lined lane (a bit claustrophobic in autumn, but better in spring after the farmer has cut back the hedgerows) until you reach the road; turn right, then left and follow the road down to the canal.
[Total miles to date = 9.5]

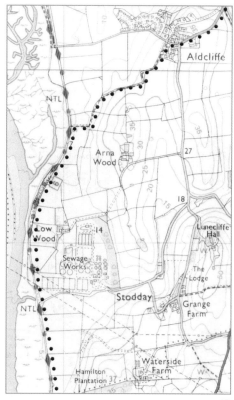

the right across the road to Christ Church, a mid-nineteenth century building on the side of the canal.]

[9-4] Follow the coastal path over the river Conder to the Conder Green picnic area, near the former Conder Green station. (There is a cafe here, and also public conveniences). The route is tree-lined and well supplied with benches and birdwatchers' arm rests!

There are pleasant views of the estuary, but little is seen inland for the trees (in

10 Lancaster Canal at Aldcliffe to Carnforth
[9 miles]

The route is along the towpath of the Lancaster Canal all the way to Carnforth, so no route map is provided for this stretch.

Ordnance Survey map: **Explorer OL41, OL7**

Public transport: Lancaster has a train station on the main west coast line. Several bus routes use the A6 road to the south of the city; it is a short walk from the A6 to the canal at Aldcliffe. To Carnforth, you can travel from Preston, Barrow, etc by train; or there are buses from Preston, Lancaster, Barrow, etc..

From Aldcliffe, walk along the canal towards Lancaster, where you can visit Lancaster Priory Church, and the locations of two former hospitals and Lancaster Friary.

Lancaster Priory
OS Map Reference: SD 47375 61996
Access: no remains of the priory visible, but access to the Priory Church;
see http://www.lancasterpriory.org/

Priory Church, Lancaster

The Benedictine priory of St Mary in Lancaster was founded around 1094 by Roger of Poitou; from finds made underneath the priory church there may have been a previous monastery on the site.

St Mary's Priory was an alien priory, i.e. dependent on a foreign monastery, in this case St Martin de Sees, in Normandy; when established there were five monks, three priests, two clerks, and servants. When the alien priories were dissolved by Act of Parliament in 1414, Lancaster Priory came into the possession of Syon Abbey in Middlesex in 1428, and remained a cell of this abbey until the general Dissolution.

The priory had granges (outlying farms) in several places including Overton, Poulton and Heaton. The church in Lancaster was granted to the abbey, as were other churches including Bolton-le-Sands, Heysham, Melling, Preston, Kirkham, Croston and Childwall; under this system about a third of the income of a church went to the incumbent, while the remainder went to the priory or abbey. King John was among those who gave lands to the priory: "...all these things I grant and confirm to the honour of God and St Mary of Lancaster for the sustenance of the monks who celebrate the service to God and St Mary in the same monastery...".

The British Library holds, in its Harley collection, a manuscript cartulary of the priory from the second quarter of the fifteenth century (Harley 3764).

The priory was situated on elevated ground (in a similar way to the other Benedictine priories of Penwortham and Upholland) alongside the castle, an unusual position as abbeys and priories more often find lower ground nearer to a source of water; but the monks must have thought themselves privileged to wake up in the morning and relish such spectacular views in each direction, including those of the hills of the Lake District to the north, which must have uplifted their spirits on their way to sing Prime!

"...there is in it a good garden and a pond in it wth a little jsland on wch an apple tree grows.."

There are no visible remains of the priory, as any remains would be under the present church - built mainly in 15th century - and in the grounds to the north of the church. In the eighteenth century, the area was described thus by Celia Fiennes:
"there has been a monastery, the walls of part of it remaine and some of ye Carv'd stones and ffigures; there is in it a good garden and a pond in it wth a little jsland on wch an apple tree grows- a Jenitin; and Strawberys all round its Rootes and ye banks of the Little jsle. There are 2 pretty wells and a vault that Leads a great way under ground

up as farre as ye Castle, wch is a good distance."

The church has been a wholly parish church since 1430 and thus escaped destruction at the Dissolution. Of particular importance inside the church are the ornate choir stalls which date from the mid-fourteenth century and thus would have been used by the monks.

It was thought the stalls may have been moved from Cockersand Abbey, but this is by no means certain; Tracy argues that Lancaster would have been quite able to pay for new choir furniture of its own.

Pevsner describes the choir stalls as having 'about the most luxuriant canopies in the country'. More elaborate furniture, cubicles in dormitories, glazed windows in the cloister to give more protection while studying and, later, rooms set aside for studying, were all developments in some monastic houses during the later medieval period. (For sources of information on Lancaster Priory, see Appendix 1 and Appendix 15).

Lancaster Friars
OS Map Reference: SD 47930 61650
Access: no remains visible.

The Dominican Friars' community was established in Lancaster around 1260 by Sir Hugh Harrington, and various traces of the friary remain, including footings of walls, in the Sulyard Street/Dalton Square area. The friary house was occupied at least until 1783. A square buttressed tower is shown on a mid-16th century sketch of Lancaster.

Also known as the Black Friars and as the Order of Preachers, the order's principal role was to defend and teach

Catholic truth; they were not tied to a particular monastery. They made, and continue to make, 'the whole world their cloister' (http://english.op.org). In September 1291, the friars were instructed by the Archbishop of York to preach the Crusade on Holy Cross Day in Lancaster, Kendal and Lonsdale. There were 30 friars in the friary in 1301. At its dissolution in 1539, the friary was sold (along with those at Preston and Warrington) to Thomas Holcroft for

Dominican Friary Reminder

£126-10-0 on 18th June 1540. Also in Lancaster, Tanner speaks of a Franciscan Convent (Grey Friars), near the bridge. (For sources of information on Lancaster Friars, see Appendix 1 and Appendix 16).

Lancaster Hospitals
OS Map Reference: St Leonard's Hospital SD 48176 62116
Access: no remains

The site of the hospital is located on modern day Bulk Road; the hospital was established by John of Mortain (later King John) around 1189 - 1194, as a leper hospital. In 1356 it was granted to Seton Nunnery near Bootle, north of Millom in Cumbria.

In the fourteenth century it supported a chaplain and nine poor persons, of whom three had to be lepers. In 1323 each person 'shall have a loaf per day which shall weigh the 8th part of a stone', with potage on Sunday, Monday and Friday.

The hospital was dissolved around 1470 - an inquiry of 1531 found that no alms had been given for 60 years, the leper house pulled down and the church and other buildings allowed to fall into ruin. There are no remains today, as the site is completely built over. The site is recorded on the first edition 1:10000 OS map.

OS Map Reference: Gardiner's Hospital SD 48176 62116
Access: no remains; an inscribed stone marks the site.

The hospital was established as an almshouse in St Mary's Gate in 1485 by the executors of the will of John Gardiner of Bailrigg. The almshouses were rebuilt in 1792, and in 1938 four almshouses were erected in Queen Street to replace those in St Mary's Gate, which were sold and the site built upon - an inscribed stone in the cottage wall marks the site. A photograph of the almshouses around 1900 can be found on 'Lancashire Lantern'.

The headship of the hospital was combined with the incumbency of a chantry in the adjacent parish church; the chantry priest was required to pay 1d per day to each of four poor people in the almshouse and 2d a week to a serving maid. The chantry was dissolved in 1547 when the hospital's income was over £11. (For sources of information on Lancaster Hospitals, see Appendix 1 and Appendix 17).

Return to the canal and head north. Once out of the built-up area, the canal veers left along the magnificent 213 year old aqueduct, designed by John Rennie, over the river Lune.

From the aqueduct you have a lovely view of the wide sweep of the river to the distant hills. [Before the canal points north again, you may wish to visit the remains of St Patrick's Chapel, and St Peter's Church, Heysham. The chapel has been dated to the 8th or 9th century, and the church has pre-Conquest stonework, including an Anglo-Saxon doorway. It is thought that an early medieval monastic community may have existed here.]

It is a pleasant walk along the canal through the fields and just before Hest Bank the sand/sea comes into view on the far left. From here the road, rail and canal travel close to each other up to Carnforth. The canal passes the edge of Bolton-le-Sands, and thence to Carnforth. Leave the canal at Carnforth near the children's playground and walk down to the main A6. [Total miles to date = 18.5]

11 Carnforth Station to Arnside Station
[8 miles]

Ordnance Survey map: **Explorer OL7**
Public transport: you can travel by train from Preston, Barrow, etc to Carnforth railway station; or take a bus from Preston, Lancaster, and Barrow. Arnside station is on the same railway line.

Carnforth Station

[11-1] Starting from the main A6 in Carnforth, walk down Market Street passing the bookshop (on your right), and you may wish to have a 'brief encounter' with Carnforth Station (http://www.carnforthstation.co.uk/) on the left; this has a Visitors' Centre, exhibitions, refreshments, etc.

Pass the station walking along Warton Road, under the first bridge and immediately before the next bridge take the road to the left (signposted a cycleway); this road runs parallel with the river Keer. Take the footbridge on the right over the river (joining the Lancashire Coastal Path) and walk alongside the old railway sidings. At the end of the sidings (Sand Lane), turn right over the bridge and towards the main road. At the road, carry straight on in the direction of Warton, over the brow of the hill; halfway down the hill, take the path on the left by the farm and follow the path along the side of a field up to the road.

Turn left along the road (Crag Road); there is little traffic along here, and you get some wonderful views looking to the south.[11-2] At its end, the road meets New Road.

'[If the tide is in, continue along the path over Heald Brow, until you reach the road; turn left along the road].

If the tide is out, turn left along the edge of the wood, reaching Brown's Houses and Jenny Brown's Point.'

Follow the road towards the railway, and as the road veers to the right, take the path directly towards a railway bridge. After the bridge, turn immediately right, through a gate, and walk along an embankment as far as Heald Brow. [If the tide is in, continue along the path over Heald Brow, until you reach the road; turn left along the road]. If the tide is out, turn left along the edge of the wood, reaching Brown's Houses and Jenny Brown's Point.

Walk along the road, see Lindeth Tower on the left; at the road junction, carry straight on through part of Silverdale village.

[11-3] As the road bends to the right after Shore Road, take the path on the left - this takes you across fields with fine views over the sea/sand.

[11-4] A track leads you up to the road - go straight on (away from Elmslack) and as the road bends to the left, take the path straight ahead into a caravan park. Walk along the path through the park, veering

to the right (not left to Far Arnside), pass toilets, then look for a way-marker pointing left down to Arnside Tower (http://www.visitcumbria.com/?s=arnside+tower&searchsubmit=U).

After visiting the tower, walk through the farmyard and on to the road. Cross over and take the path through Arnside Knott Wood. There are various ways through the wood and out the other side to Arnside. [Total miles to date = 26.5].

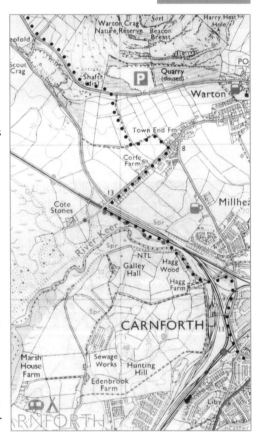

Map: 11-1

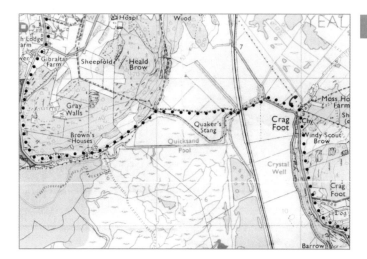

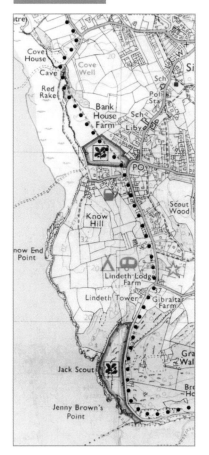

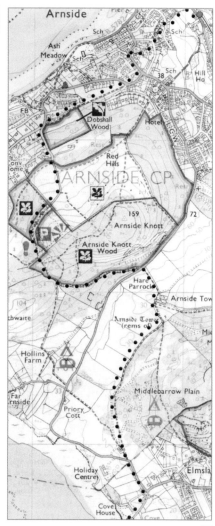

12 Arnside Station via Cartmel and Cark to Ulverston Station

[5 miles (Walking only)]

Ordnance Survey map: Explorer OL7, OL6

Public transport: trains from Barrow, Lancaster, Preston etc.

[12-1] Take the train from Arnside station to Grange over Sands. From Grange station walk left towards the village centre and at the first mini roundabout, take the right turn signposted Windermere. Walk up the road and as the road bends left, take the signed footpath on the left into the woods.

Infrequent 'Cisterian Way' Sign

On meeting the first track, there is the first signpost for the Cistercian Way (http://www.english-lakes.com/cistercian_way.htm); there are very few signs along the Way!

The footpath is marked with yellow way-markers and occasionally signs to Hampsfell. It is an uphill track all the way.

Make your way up through the woods for a considerable time, until reaching a stile in a wall at the end of the wood. Take the path ahead signposted to the Hospice and make your way, veering to your left, up to the highest point where you find the Hospice - a shelter for travellers with a lookout platform on top (http://www.visitcumbria.com/?s=Hampsfell+hospice&searchsubmit=U).

From here you have dramatic views all round, from the pencils of light on the coast to the majestic hills of the Lake District, and the first wonderful views of Cartmel with a background of hills, and Cartmel Sands to the left. In words from the Hospice:

'Then (turning to the West) is seen

Dear Cartmel's peaceful valley green

Mid waving woods and verdant lands

The fine old church of Cartmel stands

Within whose walls in days of yore

His priestly rule the prior bore....'

Cartmell from Hampsfell

You can just imagine pilgrims of medieval times getting a first view of the magnificent priory church, being greeted by the peace-

54

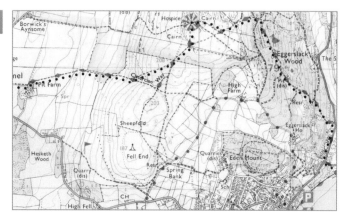

ful scene and the ringing of tuneful bells. However, the peace of the scene was rather spoilt the first day I went as Cartmel Races were in full swing, so the bells' peals were drowned by the loudspeakers from the race announcer!

From the Hospice, make your way down the obvious path in a westerly direction; after a short time take the path to the right between two hills in the direction of Cartmel, through a field and across another, aiming at Pit Farm.

Turn left at the track and almost immediately right along the edge of a field

Cartmel Priory
OS Map Reference: SD 37980 78791
Access: the Priory Church is open daily; contact by phone 01539 536261, or see http://www.cartmelpriory.org.uk/Home.

'...The impressive Priory Church survived the Dissolution in the sixteenth century and is still a beautiful place of worship...'

The Augustinian Priory of St Mary the Virgin at Cartmel was founded by William Marshall between 1189 and 1194. The impressive Priory Church survived

to a new gate. Walk through to the road (where there is a signpost for the Cistercian Way!) and into this quaint village with its impressive priory church.

Medieval Misericord, Cartmell Priory

the Dissolution in the sixteenth century and is still a beautiful place of worship for the local people and the many who visit it from far and wide.

The south part of the church had always been set aside for the use of parishioners; after the Dissolution they purchased the whole church from the Duchy of Lancaster. At the time of the Dissolution in 1536 there were 10 canons and 38 servants; unfortunately for some of the canons they became involved in the Pilgrimage of Grace and were later executed.

This independent priory normally housed 10 canons. A cell was established at Kilrush, Kildare, in Ireland in 1201-2, in order to oversee the estates granted to the priory in that country. One of its more unusual obligations was to provide guides for travellers crossing the nearby Cartmel Sands and Kent Sands.

At some stage the cloister was moved from the south side of the church to the north; some evidence for this remains on the walls of the south and north sides of the church. An excavation in 1983 on the north side of the church revealed part of the Augustinian cemetery.

Pevsner describes the top stage of the tower, at an angle of 45 degrees, as a 'structurally dubious but visually entertaining motif'. The priory gatehouse, built around 1340, still exists. (For sources of information on Cartmel Priory, see Appendix 1 & Appendix 18).

[12-2] From the priory walk west up the main street and head for Cartmel Park (race track). Follow the path through the car park; the path veers gently left, through two fields used for horse-riding training. Pass Seven Acres farm (abandoned) on your right, through a gate into Lane Park wood.

'This is a very quiet and scenic road with a valley on the left and woods on the right.'

This track looks like an old road, with walls on either side; follow this track through the wood and out the other side. After about a hundred yards, the track forks - take the left fork on to a narrow, tarmaced road. This is a very quiet and scenic road with a valley on the left and woods on the right. On reaching the main road, turn right and walk into Cark village.

Keep left over the river by the pub, pass a small supermarket and carry on up the road over the railway and turn left into the railway yard to catch the train to Ulverston (every two hours). Nearby is the church of St John the Baptist, Flookburgh (http://www.carlislediocese.org. uk/our-churches/parishes-clergy/windermere/9032.html).

The train from Cark to Ulverston takes you over Cartmel Sands, where you can see Chapel Island in the middle of the estuary on your left.
[Total miles to date = 31.5].

Map: 12-2

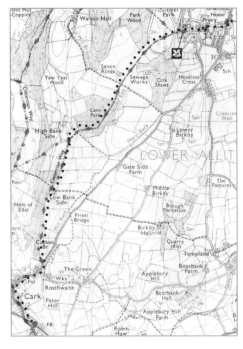

13 Ulverston Station to Conishead Priory and back
[8 miles]

Ordnance Survey map: **Explorer OL6, OL7**

Public transport: trains to Ulverston from Barrow, Lancaster, Preston etc. Bus service No. 11 runs along the main road by Conishead Priory.

[13-1] Conishead Priory is well worth a visit; the original priory is long gone and nothing remains, but the nineteenth century building is now a Buddhist centre and Temple.

You can walk to it directly from Ulverston station using roads, but a little longer walk can be taken away from the roads using the man-made Ulverston Canal and part of the Cumbria Coastal Way (Cumbria Coastal Way (http://www.visitcumbria.com/wc/the-cumbria-coastal-way/).

From Station Approach, turn left towards the town and on reaching the main A590 (County Road), turn right along it, over a couple of junctions/roundabouts until you reach Canal Head (from the station to Canal Head is very busy and noisy!). On the canal, the towpath is on the north side, with industries along almost the whole length of the south side.

The canal is approximately 1.3 miles long and as straight as an arrow. At Canal Foot you join the Cumbria Coastal Way; cross over the former sea lock and head along the road in a south-westerly direction. After about half a mile, as the road bends to the right, take the track to the left, passing some small firms along the way.

Eventually go through a gate on the left (with Cumbria Coastal Way sign on it) diagonally right across the field with horses grazing, through a gate and head in

a straight line, between some newish farm buildings and meet a narrow road. After about 250 yards the road bends to the left and on the right is a permissive way through the woods to Conishead Priory.

> '...the original priory is long gone and nothing remains, but the nineteenth century building is now a Buddhist centre and Temple.'

Map: 13-1

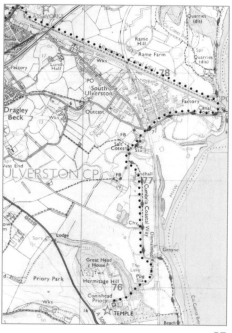

57

Conishead Priory
OS Map Reference: SD 30460 75790
Access: open to the public daily throughout
the year; see
http://www.conisheadpriory.org/
or phone 01229 584029.

Conishead Priory, an Augustinian house dedicated to St Mary, replaced a leper hospital which had been founded between 1154 and 1158; the hospital was dissolved in 1181 when it became a priory.

Because of its proximity to Furness Abbey, there were disputes with that house, but they were settled amicably, with Conishead agreeing to limit the number of canons to 13, unless agreement was forthcoming from Furness to increase that figure.

'At the Dissolution in 1536, there were eight canons, plus an ex-prior with a pension, and one canon serving at Orton Church...'

At the Dissolution in 1536, there were eight canons, plus an ex-prior with a pension, and one canon serving at Orton Church; there were also 37 servants. Among the churches held by the priory were Pennington in Furness, Muncaster and Whitbeck in Cumberland, Orton in Westmorland, Poulton in Lonsdale, Ulverston and Ponsonby in Cumberland. Its income at the Dissolution was £97, raised to £161-5-9 by the Commissioners. The priory did not forget the poor, giving £9 per year to help them.

Nothing remains of the original priory. The existing house, now part of a Buddhist monastery (and thus continuing the role of the site as a place of prayer), was built between 1821 and 1836, replacing the previous building.

The foundations of the original priory church were found in 1823 under the lawn to the south of the present building and excavations took place in 1928. It was found that the church was cruciform in shape and built of yellow sandstone, with a 100ft long nave; there were no aisles.

A plan produced at the time of the excavations revealed 13th century foundations for the chancel arch, nave arch and part of the nave wall. It is believed that stone from the destroyed priory was used to rebuild parts of Ulverston Church.

(For sources of information on Conishead Priory, see Appendix 1 and Appendix 19).

To return to the Cistercian Way, there are a number of options; the one chosen here is to return to Ulverston station the same way, for logistical reasons.

[The alternatives are:
a. return the same way [4 miles];
b. return to the station via the main road [2 miles];
c. if you are continuing the walk, go along the main road in the direction of Ulverston, pass the Lodge on the right and after about 300 yards take the path on the left near Gascow Farm. Near Highfield Farm the path turns to the right.

After a further two fields you reach a junction; turn right, and then left at The Grange. On reaching the road, turn right

> **Dogs Found Chasing Livestock Will Be Shot**

Unfortunate for dogs that cannot read

and almost immediately take the path on the left towards The Nook Farm. Go through the farm and soon turn left to reach the road and rejoin the Cistercian Way; turn left. 2.25 miles].

[Total miles to date = 39.5 (using option a.)]

14 Ulverston Station to Furness Abbey

[8 miles]

Ordnance Survey map: **Explorer OL6**

Public transport: trains to Ulverston from Barrow, Lancaster, Preston etc. Stations nearest to Furness Abbey are Dalton-in-Furness and Barrow-in-Furness. Buses run to both on the main road outside the abbey.

There is mention in the Furness Coucher book of a leper hospital in or near Ulverston in 1247, but the location is unknown [14-1].

From Ulverston Station, leave Station Approach and turn right. After a short distance take the footpath to the right, signposted Swarthmoor Hall. Follow the path over a stream, straight ahead over a field to a gate and track which takes you to Swarthmoor Hall, owned by the Society of Friends, and recognised as the centre of the beginning of Quakerism; George Fox lived there (http://www.

Swarthmoor Hall

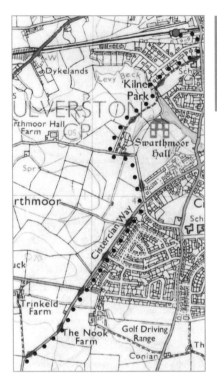

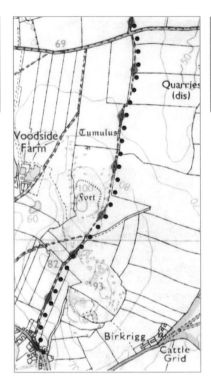

swarthmoorhall.co.uk/). On reaching the road, turn left and follow the road until it reaches the main road, at which turn right.

The road becomes less busy after passing the houses on the left. [14-2] On reaching a 'T' junction, take the footpath directly opposite - a little overgrown to start with but you soon reach the edge of the field. Head up over fields, keeping left of a hill fort. Look back for a lovely view of the estuary, the surrounding hills and mountains of the Lake District in the distance. You soon reach a track and head down directly to Great Urswick, aiming for the church ((http://www.urswickchurch.co.uk/index. html) - you can walk either way round Urswick Tarn.

[14-3] There is a path behind the church which crosses two fields, and then turns sharp right in the next field to take you back to the road. Here you can either take path due south to the stream, then sharp right back to the road; or walk along the

road to the centre of the village.

Once in the village, follow the path between the houses - signed to Little Urswick Crags. The path is not well signed or obvious, but head up towards the crags. At a stile in a wall, take the left hand path (which is signed), walk alongside the wall and find another stile; go directly across the field to meet a track; turn right along the track.

In early May the sides of this track are covered in wild garlic, bluebells and the occasional primrose.

[Alternatively, you can go straight ahead over the crags and make for a gate on the far side of the field; follow the track straight ahead to the road and turn left.

When you reach a fork in the road, take the right hand fork and after about 150 yards, take the path on right along side of field]. [14-4] Keep going straight ahead,

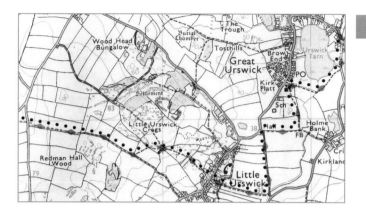

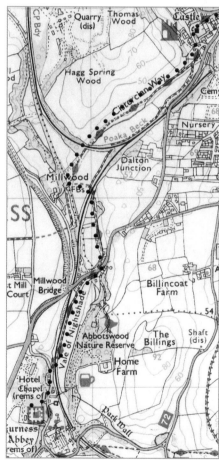

Church of St Mary, Great Urswick (left) & Dalton Castle (right)

following this path through several fields until you reach a road; cross the road, go straight ahead over a short field and cross the next road into the field opposite. [14-5]

After the first field, go straight ahead to cross two new stiles, probably watched intently by horses and sheep! From the second stile walk slightly right into the dip, where you find another stile. Head straight up and across the field making for a stile in the top left-hand corner of field.

Turn right along the road and after 40 yards take the path across the field on your left. Walk down and then along the path parallel with the railway; walk through the tunnel under the railway and make your way to the main road in Dalton-in-Furness.

[A rare Cistercian Way symbol marker here!]

Pass the Catholic Church (Our Lady of the Rosary and St Margaret of Scotland), the Seventh-Day Adventist Church and the

United Reformed Church, towards Dalton Castle http://www.nationaltrust.org.uk/main/w-daltoncastle; http://www.visitcumbria.com/sl/dalton-castle/) and the Church at the top of the main road.

Take the road behind the church and, before reaching the beck, take the footpath to the right along a pleasant valley.

Eventually you walk under the railway line, and before reaching the wood, take the little footbridge on the left and head straight across the field and pass under another railway line; follow the track to the main road. Cross directly over the road (there is a dangerous bend here, so it may be safer to cross further along the road), taking the path along the Valley of Nightshade, with Abbotswood Nature Reserve on your left.

Cross under the railway and make for the road - with one of the gateways into Furness Abbey in front of you.

[Total miles for Section Two = **47.5**]

Furness Abbey
OS Map Reference: SD 21826 71782
http://www.english-heritage.org.uk/visit/
places/furness-abbey/ , http://www.furness-
abbey.org.uk/home%20page.html

The last monastery on this journey
through old Lancashire is the grandest,
both in its pre-Dissolution form, and
in terms of what remains today - only
Whalley Abbey coming anywhere near it
on these counts.

The abbey of St Mary moved to Furness
to the 'vale of the nightshade', sometimes called the Vale of Bekanesgill, from
Tulketh in Preston in 1127, founded by
Stephen, Count of Boulogne and Mortain and Lord of Lancaster. Originally a
Savigniac abbey, it was absorbed within
the Cistercian order in 1147.

Like all Cistercian abbeys, it followed
the Rule of St Benedict, was relatively
secluded, and pursued a strict, simple
way of life; in these early days manual
labour was an important part of the

First view of Furness Abbey

monk's day, along with prayer, study and
celebration of the liturgy.

The abbey grew to be the largest in
Lancashire; its original grants included
Furness, Walney Island and the manor of
Ulverston, but later further possessions
were granted in Lancashire, Yorkshire
and the Isle of Man; these included
granges in Stalmine, Beaumont and
Hawkshead - the building in the last is
still in existence (IOE No 76835).

Income was derived also from the rectories of Dalton, Hawkshead, Urswick and Millom. The value of the abbey in 1535 was over £805, it being the second richest Cistercian house after Fountains Abbey. It was dissolved on 9 April 1537.

The abbey fulfilled its responsibility to the local community in several ways, including providing meat and drink for children and labourers, and providing a school.

The abbey also kept thirteen poor men as almsmen; and every year bread and meat were given out at the gate, and it also helped local widows. The cellarer, according to Benedict's Rule, is asked to: "...provide for the sick, the children, the guests, and the poor, with all care". Of the remains, Pevsner says that:

'much stands and...in such a fashion that it makes the ruin, in the warm colour of its red sandstone, one of the finest in England'.

The abbey also retains 'one of the best ensembles of sedilia and piscina anywhere in England'.

Despite the passage of nearly five hundred years, the remains are extensive, including much of the church of St Mary, the chapter house, infirmary, part of the cloister, and several other buildings. (For sources of information on Furness Abbey, see Appendix 1 and Appendix 20).

[Total miles
for Sections One & Two =

117]

Other Lancashire monastic houses

(not included in this walk)

Barnoldswick Abbey
OS Map Reference: SD 87290 46680

Another short-lived monastic establishment in modern Lancashire (in Yorkshire in medieval times), the Cistercian abbey of Mount St Mary's at Barnoldswick was founded by Henry de Lacy on 19th May 1147, but was transferred to Kirkstall in 1152, owing to poor land and problems from robbers; the site became a grange of Kirkstall Abbey.

It was founded from Fountains Abbey by an abbot, with 12 monks and 10 lay brothers (conversi). The exact site is unknown, but is reputed to be in a field called Monkroyd (Monk's Cross), on Calf Hall Lane.

(For sources of information on Barnoldswick Abbey, see Appendix 1 and Appendix 21).

Hornby Priory
OS Map Reference: SD 57740 69030

The Premonstratensian Priory of St Wilfrid at Hornby was a dependent cell of Croxton Abbey in Leicestershire. It was founded around 1172 by the Montbegon family; it was on a site that was possibly used earlier as an eighth-century church or monastery. The priory may have begun as a hospital after 1160. In 1535 the priory is recorded as giving alms to thirteen poor people; it was dissolved in 1538.

(For sources of information on Hornby Priory, see Appendix 1).

Kersal Cell
OS Map Reference: SD 35670 27970

A cell of Cluniac monks dedicated to St Leonard was established in Kersal, Broughton, Salford, the mother house being in Lenton near Nottingham; the date was sometime between 1143 and 1153. Cluniac monks followed the Rule of St Benedict, with the celebration of the liturgy being central to their lives. The cell at Kersal never seems to have had more than a prior and one or two monks.

A house, still standing, was built on the site of the priory in the sixteenth century; its foundations are those of the original priory, and it may have used part of the priory in its early construction.

(For sources of information on Kersal Cell, see Appendix 1).

Lytham Priory

OS Map Reference: SD 35670 27970

The Benedictine Priory at Lytham was a cell of Durham Priory, and founded by Richard of Woodplumpton between 1189 and 1194, being dedicated to St Mary and St Cuthbert. The priory had lands in Lytham, Carleton and nearby, and also in Appleby in Leicestershire. It usually had three monks plus a prior, so was very small. The priory was dissolved in 1534/5.

Nothing remains of the priory; more than one hall was built on the site, the current Lytham Hall having been completed in 1764/7.

(For sources of information on Lytham Priory, see Appendix 1 and Appendix 21).

Warrington Friars

OS Map Reference: SJ 60620 87950

This Augustinian friary, occupying a site near Bridge Street and Friars Gate in the centre of the town, was established in the thirteenth century, possibly taking over a former hospital. Augustinian (Austin) Friars followed the rule of St Augustine, whom they regarded as their spiritual founder, and became a preaching order. The Friary in Warrington was surrendered in 1539 and sold, along with the friaries at Preston and Lancaster, to Thomas Holcroft. The church remained in use after the Dissolution, at least until the seventeenth century; excavations in 1981 provided evidence that the domestic buildings of the friary were demolished in the early seventeenth century.

Earlier excavations in 1886 found remains of the choir and nave - there is a photograph on the Warrington Museum's website - http://www.warringtonmuseum.co.uk/collections/local-history/

(For sources of information on Warrington Friary, see Appendix 1 and Appendix 21).

Wyresdale Abbey

OS Map Reference: SD 56100 54200 ?

The Cistercian Abbey of Wyresdale, at modern-day Abbeystead, was shortlived - it was established around 1193-1196 probably by Theobald Walter with monks from Furness Abbey, but by 1204 the community had moved to Ireland. The church of St Michael on Wyre was appropriated to the new monastery. There are no remains of the abbey, and the exact location is yet to be discovered; on the first edition 6" to one mile map, the site lies north-east of the present Abbeystead reservoir.

(For sources of information on Wyresdale Abbey, see Appendix 1 and Appendix 21).

Part Two
(the sources)

Appendices 1 - 21

The more general sources are given in Appendix 1, and the other Appendices cover more particular sources for each individual monastery. Appendix 1 includes information on library and archive catalogues and other sources from both local and national authorities, and sources such as the Victoria County History of Lancashire, books by Marshall, Knowles, Dugdale, and Tanner; the Valor Ecclesiasticus, and cartularies on several monasteries.

The Appendices list sources of information in reverse-chronological order of the original text, as far as is feasible; e.g. cartularies will be listed in the medieval period rather than when they were reprinted. A repository, or a website address, for the full-text of the source is generally given after the source detail, e.g. [LCL] indicates that a copy of the book can be found in the Lancashire County Library - look at the Lancashire County Library Online Catalogue (see Appendix 1 for web address) for the book's exact location. There may be locations for the item in other libraries and repositories.

Abbreviations:
CAS - Cumbria Archives Service
CASB - Cumbria Archives Service, Barrow
CASK - Cumbria Archives Service, Kendal
CCL - Cumbria County Library
EHNMR - English Heritage National Monuments Record

HLP - Harris Library, Preston
LCL - Lancashire County Library
LCLDL - Lancashire County Library Digital Library
LL - Lancashire Lantern
LRO - Lancashire Record Office
WL - Warrington Library

Appendix I

General Sources

21st Century

Lancashire County Council's group of databases:

Lancashire County Library Catalogue - www.lancashire.gov.uk/libraries/

Lancashire County Library Digital Library - http://www.lancashire.gov.uk/libraries-and-archives/libraries/digital-library.aspx

Lancashire Lantern (http://www.lantern.lancashire.gov.uk). Includes an image database, and an index to local newspapers.

Lancashire Record Office (http://www.lancashire.gov.uk/libraries-and-archives/archives-and-record-office.aspx). Includes online catalogues to records.

Lancashire Historic Environment Record: 01772 533404.

History of the priory or abbey, including detailed description of any remains. Lists documentary sources up to the present time. Geology of the area. Details of any excavations.

MARIO (Maps and Related Information Online)
http://mario.lancashire.gov.uk/.

Includes current (based on Ordnance Survey), historical and aerial maps.

Cumbria County Council's group of databases:

Cumbria Library Catalogue (http://cmbr.ent.sirsidynix.net.uk/client/default)

Cumbria Archives Catalogue -
(http://www.cumbria.gov.uk/archives/Online_catalogues/default.asp)

Cumbria Image Collection (http://www.cumbriaimagebank.org.uk/)

English Heritage group of online databases on historic buildings and sites:

National Monuments Record (NMR) (http://pastscape.english-heritage.org.uk/)
Gives descriptions and history of sites and buildings, lists any excavations or surveys that have taken place, and gives links to maps and other websites.

Images of England (http://www.imagesofengland.org.uk/) Gives images and text for most of the listed buildings in England; the text is mainly architectural information about the buildings.

English Heritage Archives (http://www.englishheritagearchives.org.uk/).
Photographs and documents on England's historic buildings and archaeological sites.

Heritage Gateway (http://www.heritagegateway.org.uk/gateway/) Searches across national and local records of England's historic sites and buildings. e.g. leads to listed buildings (information similar to 'Images of England' data); to NMR's Pastscape, and to NMR Excavation Index.

Viewfinder (http://viewfinder.english-heritage.org.uk/)
Photographs from 1850s held on the NMR.

National Archives, including Duchy of Lancaster papers:
(http://www.nationalarchives.gov.uk/default.htm).
'Discovery' database holds more than 32 million descriptions of records held by The National Archives and more than 2,500 archives across the country. Use ful information also at http://www.duchyoflancaster.co.uk

British Library group of online catalogues, including the main Explore the British Library Catalogue (http://explore.bl.uk/primo_library/libweb/action/search.do?dscnt=1&dstmp=1

4438536251111&vid=BLVU1&fromLogin=true)

Historic Society of Lancashire and Cheshire. Index to Transactions - http://www.hslc.org.uk/index_search.php?section=23&type=index

Cumberland and Westmorland Antiquarian and Archaeological Society. Index to Transactions -

http://cumbriapast.com/cgi-bin/ms/main.pl?action=transindex

Online bibliographic databases, including Historical Abstracts, Social Scisearch, British Humanities Index, etc. [ProQuest Dialog, etc]

Kerr, Julie. Health and Safety in the Medieval Monasteries of Britain. History, 93:309, 2008, p. 3-19. [EBSCOHost]

Marshall, Brian. Lancashire's medieval monasteries. Blackpool : Landy Publishing, 2006. ISBN 1872895689. [LCL]

20th Century

Leading the way : a history of Lancashire's roads, edited by A.G. Crosby. Lancashire County Books, 1998. ISBN 1871236339. Includes information about ancient routes, including those near monastic houses; cartularies of monastic houses state that certain roads existed at set times, e.g. Cockersand. Includes references. [LCL]

Hindle, Paul. Roads and Tracks of the Lake District. Cicerone Press, 1998. ISBN 1852842598. Detailed look at roads from Roman times, including sand routes, corpse roads etc. [LCL, CCL]

Clark, M.A. Reformation in the Far North: Cumbria and the Church, 1500-1571. Northern History Vol 32, Jan 1996, p 75-89. [EBSCOHost]

Frith, May. The monasteries : houses of God or dens of vice?: the facts detailed in Lancashire but applicable to the whole country. Blackpool & Fylde Historical Soc. for M.W. Frith, 1995. Attempts to look at the facts and give a balanced view of monasteries in 1530s. [LCL]

Coppack, Glyn. English Heritage book of abbeys and priories. Batsford, 1990. 147876 ISBN 0713463082 0713463090 [LCL]

Brodie, Ian O. The Cistercian Way : a South Lakeland walk : the official guide. Carnegie P, 1989. ISBN 094878931X. [LCL]

Ordnance Survey. Roman Britain. Edition [4th ed.] Scale 1:625,000 or about 1" to 10 miles. O.S, 1978. 2 maps, "Roman Britain: North sheet", "Roman Britain: South sheet", held in front pocket. South sheet shows roads: Ribchester - East (Elslack, Ilkley...) and West (Kirkham and beyond); North (Burrow in Lonsdale and beyond) and South (Manchester). Possible route Walton-le-Dale - South and North (to Lancaster, thence to join Burrow in Lonsdale road. [LCL]

Sagar, Peter. Lancashire monasteries. [1974-5] Articles from the "Nelson Local History Newsletter", nos. 25, 26, 27, 28, 29, 31 and 34, Jan 1974-Feb. 1975. [LCL]

Knowles, David. Medieval religious houses, England and Wales, by David Knowles and R. Neville Hadcock. Longman, 1971. 0582112303. Lists individual priories, etc. Groups Orders together. [LCL]

Pevsner, Nikolaus. Lancashire. 2, The rural north. Buildings of England Series. Penguin, 1969. ISBN 014071037X. [LCL]

Chetham Society. Remains... 3rd series, Vol. 17 : The last days of the Lancashire monasteries and the pilgrimage of grace, by Christopher Haigh. Good overview. Good bibliography, listing primary sources (manuscript and printed), and secondary sources. Manchester U.P. for C.S, 1969. [LCL]

Knowles, David. The monastic order in England : a history of its development from the times of St. Dunstan to the Fourth Lateran Council 940-1216. 2nd ed. C.U.P, 1963. [LCL]

Matthew, Donald. The Norman monasteries and their English possessions. Series Historical series: second series. O.U.P., 1962. [LCL]

Davis, G. R. C. Medieval cartularies of Great Britain : a short catalogue. Longmans, Green, 1958. Dated, but good detail for each monastic house; includes references to transcriptions by Societies etc where relevant. Includes Burscough, Cockersand, Furness, Lancaster Priory, Lytham, Penwortham (under Evesham), Preston Hospital, Sawley and Whalley. [LCL]

Ordnance Survey. Map of monastic Britain: south sheet. Scale 1:625,000. Publisher Ordnance Survey, 1950. [LCL]

Knowles, David. The religious orders in England. [Vol. 1, The old orders 1216-1340, the Friars 1216-1340, the monasteries and their world]. C.U.P, 1948. [Vol.2, The end of the Middle Ages]. [Vol.3, The Tudor age]. [LCL]

Bradley, Edith. The story of the English Abbeys : told in counties. Vol 1, The Northern counties. Edition 1: The Northern counties. Hale, 1938. [LCL]

Home, Beatrice. Chester, Manchester and Liverpool. Series Cathedrals, Abbeys and Famous Churches Publisher Dent, 1925. [LCL]

The VICTORIA history of the county of Lancaster. / edited by William Farrer and J. Brownbill. Series: Victoria History of the Counties of England. Constable, 1906 - . Detailed histories of religious houses, with comprehensive lists of references. [LCL] Also online at http://www.british-history.ac.uk/

19th Century

Online Directories (http://specialcollections.le.ac.uk/cdm/landingpage/collection/p16445coll4)

Local Friaries and Priories. The Preston Chronicle, Saturday, February 14, 1891. [LCLDL; also HLP].

Notes on the ancient religious houses of the County of Lancaster. Dom. G. Dolan HSLC Volume: 43 (1891-1892) Pages: 201-232 [LCL]

Dugdale, William. Monasticon Anglican : a history of the abbies and other monasteries, hospitals, frieries, and cathedral and collegiate churches, ... originally published in Latin.... New ed / by John Caley, Sir Henry Ellis and Bulkeley Bandinel. London : James Bohn, 1846. [LCL]

Camden Society. Publications of the Camden Society. [Old series, vol. 26], Three chapters of letters relating to the suppression of monasteries / edited from the originals in the British Museum by Thomas Wright. Publisher Camden Soc, 1843. [LCL]

Survey of religious houses - First and second values; Bells, lead and woods; Woods worth to be sold; No. of religious persons, their debts, servants and others, and their offer of redemption. For Cockersand, Cartmel, Conishead, Burscough and Holland "within the case of Dissolution". [Harleian Codex 604.]. Subject Baines Manuscript Collection. Handwritten transcription from "Harleian Codex 604 Folio G1".- 22 items bound in volume with cover title "Harleian series: volume I". BAI A 21 [LCL]

Baines, Edward. History, directory and gazetteer of the county palatine of Lancaster : with a variety of commercial and statistical information. Vol.1. Liverpool : London : W. Wales ; Longman, Hurst, 1824. + Vol 2. [LCL]

Greenwood's ftof Lancashire, 1818. [LCL]

Hennet's Map of Lancashire, 1829. [LCL]

18th Century

Yates' Map of Lancashire, 1786. [LCL]

The journeys of Celia Fiennes. Cresset 1949. [LCL]

Tanner, Thomas. Notitia monastica, or, An account of all the abbies, priories, and houses of friers, heretofore in England and Wales; and also of all the colleges and hospitals founded before A.D. MDXL. London : Printed by William Bowyer, at the expense of the Society for the Encouragement of Learning, 1744. (Late Lord Bishop of St Asaph). General history - origin, progress, increase pp i - xiii; orders pp xiii - xxv; abbies, priories etc incl officers pp xxv - xxxiii; Dissolution pp xxxiii - xlii. Notes on arms, by county. Catalogue of Greater Monasteries: Furness, Whalley. For each monastery, gives a short history in English, including a valuation at Dissolution; and references (in Latin) to medieval sources. Indexes: abbies, priories, etc; founders, benefactors; grantees after Dissolution; Principals of Religious Houses (only 3 from Lancashire included) [LCL]

Defoe, Daniel. A tour through the whole island of Great Britain. Vol. 1 and Vol 2. Series: Everyman's Library; 821. Dent, 1962. [LCL]

Willis, Browne. History of abbies [extract]. Baines Manuscript Collection. Handwritten extract from vol. 2 of "An history of the mitred parliamentary abbies, and conventual cathedral churches", published: London, 1719. - 1st of 21 items bound in volume with cover title "Lancashire general history". [LCL]

17th Century

DODSWORTH, Roger, and DUGDALE (Sir William) Monasticon Anglicanum sive Pandectæ Cœnobiorum, Benedictinorum Cluniacensium, Cisterciensium, Carthusianorum; a primordiis ad eorum usque dissolutionem. Per R. D. [and] G. D. (Προπυλαιον J. Marshami - Volumen Tertium et ultimum: Additamenta ... continens ... per W. Dugdale.). 3 vol. Londoni, 1655-73. [British Library - http://explore.bl.uk/primo_library/libweb/action/search.do?t=1&dstmp=1443853625111&vid=BLVU1&fromLogin=true   Speed's Map of 1610. [LCL]

16th Century

Henry VIII Letters and Papers, Foreign and Domestic, 1509 - 1547, 21 Vols. [British History website - http://www.british-history.ac.uk/subject.aspx?subject=1&gid=126]

VALOR ecclesiasticus : temp. Henr. VIII institutus. 6 Vols. [LCL]

Leland, John. John Leland's itinerary : travels in Tudor England, [edited by] John Chandler. Sutton, 1993. ISBN 086299957X [LCL]

Papal Documents. [Location: British History website - http://www.british-history.ac.uk/subject.aspx?subject=2&gid=150]

15th Century and earlier

National Archives, including Duchy of Lancaster papers: (http://www.nationalarchives.gov.uk/default.htm). 'Discovery' database holds more than 32 million descriptions of records held by The National Archives and more than 2,500 archives across the country. Useful information also at http://www.duchyoflancaster.co.uk

Papal Documents. [Location: British History website - http://www.british-history.ac.uk/subject.aspx?subject=2&gid=150]

Appendix 2

Upholland Priory

Please see **Appendix 1 - General Sources** for full details of the main sources of information, and full references. **The General Sources** are not included below

21st Century

St Thomas the Martyr Priory Church website; includes history, services, events etc. [http://www.stthomasthemartyr.org.uk]

Upholland, St Thomas, Church of. PR 3389. [LRO]

Lancashire Churches, by Tony Boughen. Includes...Upholland, etc. Includes history, and images. [http://www.lancashirechurches.co.uk/index.htm]

20th Century

The Priory Church of Saint Thomas the Martyr, Up Holland : a short descriptive and historical note.... 5th ed. Publisher Sharon P, 1987. [LCL]

The Priory Church of Saint Thomas the Martyr, Up Holland : a short descriptive and historical note first published on the occasion of the 650th anniversary of the foundation of the church. 1957. [LCL]

Wheeler- R. A. Anniversaries : the 650th anniversary of the founding of the Church of St. Thomas the Martyr- up Holland / by R. A. Wheeler. Historic Society of Lancashire & Cheshire Trans, 1957, vol. 109 1957, p 188-9. [LCL]

Upholland. St. Thomas the Martyr Priory Church. The Priory Church of St Thomas the Martyr, Upholland : letter to visitors. [LCL]

Wills, G. F. Three touches of a Lancashire parish with national history. Publisher [Liverpool : Brakell (Printers)], [1908] Subject: Upholland - Upholland Priory. Reprinted from the "Transactions of the Historic Society of Lancashire and Cheshire. Vol. 60, 1908." Three 'touches' are: The rebellion of Thomas Lancaster in reign of Edward II; The Dissolution of the Monasteries; the Great Rebellion. Photos. [LCL]

19th Century

Bray, David. The architectural history of St. Thomas the Martyr Priory Church, Upholland, 1307-1887. No date. Photocopied typescript. At foot of title page: "Originally published by the Lancashire History Quarterly". [LCL]

Liverpool Mercury (Liverpool, England), Friday, September 12, 1862. Naturalists' Field Club event at Upholland. Some history of the priory. [LCLDL; also Liverpool Library]

Priory of Holland no. 1. Subject Baines Manuscript Collection. Upholland Priory. Handwritten copy in Latin and English. Tells demise of original college etc. [LCL]

18th Century

Diary or Woodall's Register (London, England), Friday, October 15, 1790; Issue 485. Boys found silver coins in wall adjoining the remains of old Abbey. [LCLDL]

Buck's views, including Up Holland priory, etc. 1727-1728. DP 189. [LRO]

Appendix 3

Lathom Park Chapel - (St John the Divine)

Please see Appendix 1 - General Sources for full details of the main sources of information, and full references. The General Sources are not included below

21st Century
Historic Lathom : long lost Lathom discovered. Lathom Park Trust, 2004. [LCL]
Church of England, Lathom Park Chapel St John Parish, Lancs. PR3378 1855-1995 12 Files. Mainly recent. Some photos and 2 histories. [LRO].

20th Century
Hosker, P. 'The Stanleys of Lathom and ecclesiastical patronage in the north-west of England during the fifteenth century'. Northern History, 18 (1982), 212-29. Publisher: Maney. ISSN 0078172X. [LCL]
Lathom Park Chapel : short illustrated history. Includes photo of chapel and almshouses and vestries, screen, sanctuary and east window. [LCL]
Highway to Lathom. Chorley Guardian. 16-Jun-1967. [LL]
Lathom Park Chapel, St John PR 3378/14/6 "The Ancient Chapel of St John the Divine, Lathom Park 1500-1950" a guide and history by Atherton and Westhead, 1950. [LRO]
Atherton, G. B. Guide and history of the ancient chapel of Saint John the Divine in Lathom Park, founded in the year 1500, by G. B. Atherton and John Westhead. Kendal : Titus Wilson, No date. Detailed guide to chapel, plus history and list of bodies of descendants of Lord Skelmersdale removed from Skelmersdale Parish Church in 1880. [LCL]

19th century
The Late Countess of Lathom. Liverpool Mercury, Monday, November 29, 1897. Funeral etc. Mourners took the Sacrament in St John the Divine, generally known as Lathom Park Chapel. [LCLDL]
Historical sketches of Ormskirk, Ormskirk Church; Lathom House, past and present; Lord Lathom, the siege of Lathom House, and reminiscences connected therewith; Burscough Priory, etc., Ormskirk : T. Hutton, 1881. [LCL]
Miscellaneous. The Leeds Mercury (Leeds, England), Saturday, December 19, 1857. Workmen found skeletons, said to be from battle of Lathom House; 2 deposited in Chapel. (From Preston Chronicle). [LCLDL]
Foundation of Lathom Priory, Subject Baines Manuscript Collection. Handwritten transcription. [LCL]

Appendix 4

Burscough Priory

Please see Appendix 1 - General Sources for full details of the main sources of information, and full references. The General Sources are not included below

21st Century
[Walk around Burscough Priory] Merseyside Travel, 2001.

Lancashire Churches, by Tony Boughen. Includes...Ormskirk, etc. Includes history, and images. [http://www.lancashirechurches.co.uk/index.htm]

20th Century
Padfield, H. Blessed Saint Nicholas : an historical account of Burscough Priory, 1189-1536. 1968. [LCL]

[Notes re Burscough Priory]. UDOR 15/43 n.d. [c.1920]. [LRO]

Cheetham, F. H. Burscough Priory. Offprint from the "Transactions of the Lancashire & Cheshire Antiquarian Society", Vol. 26, 1908. [LCL].

19th Century
Rylands- W. Harry. Masons' marks at Burscough Priory- Ormskirk Church... and...other buildings...with notes on the general history of masons' marks / by W. Harry Rylands. Historic Society of Lancashire & Cheshire Transactions 1892 vol.43-4 1891-2 p123-300 [LCL].

Literary and Dramatic Notes. Liverpool Mercury etc (Liverpool, England), Wednesday, March 18, 1891; Issue 13477. Bromley's excavations. [LCLDL]

Bromley, James. Notes on some recent excavations at Burscough Priory. Publisher Liverpool : T. Brakell (Printer), 1890. Reprinted from "Transactions of the Historic Society of Lancashire and Cheshire", Vol. 41. pp 127-146d. [LCL]

[...] Parties Names: Notes on some Excavations at Burscough Priory DDK/128/4A 1890 [LRO]

Ormskirk, SS Peter and Paul PR 3385/14/34 Copy 1887 plan of priory of St Nicholas at Burscough Detailed plan (from 1887) of site, including church, cloister (part), almonry, etc. [LRO]

Local News. Liverpool Mercury etc. Monday, March 16, 1885. Restoration of Ormskirk Parish Church....two marble effigies from Burscough Priory [LCLDL]

Historical sketches of Ormskirk, Ormskirk Church; .... Burscough Priory, etc., Publisher Ormskirk : T. Hutton, 1881. [LCL]

Fishwick, Henry. Burscough Priory, in the County of Lancaster. Reliquary 16, Apr 1876, p. 205-208. [British Periodicals Collection, UMI]

Draper, Peter. The house of Stanley : including the sieges of Lathom House, with notices of relative and co-temporary incidents, etc. Ormskirk : Hutton, 1864. [Lancashire County Library; also excerpt at http://www.isle-of-man.com/manxnotebook/fulltext/hs1864/p313.htm

Earl of Derby. The Preston Chronicle Saturday, July 12, 1851. Burial of Earl of Derby at Ormskirk Church. [LCLDL; and HLP]

The Charities of Blackburn. The Preston Chronicle (Preston, England), Saturday, June 15, 1850. Mentions a burial at Lydiate Abbey (not really an abbey)....Funerals have taken place within Burscough Abbey 'within living memory'.... [LCLDL and HLP]

Opening of the Liverpool, Ormskirk & Preston Railway. Preston Chronicle, Saturday, April 7, 1849. Mentions proximity of Burscough Priory, '....a spot once deemed sacred from all secular intrusions...' etc [LCLDL]

Robert Fitz Henry de Lathom's grant of the Church of St Nicholas of Burscough and the Church of Flixton. Subject Baines Manuscript Collection. Burscough Priory. St Nicholas was the tutelar saint of Burscough Priory. [LCL]

Priory of Burscough: Robert Fitz Henry's foundation charter. Subject Baines Manuscript Collection. Handwritten copy of extract from Dugdale's Monasticon, vol. 1. [LCL].

18th Century

Seal of the Priory Church of Burscough, Lancashire. British Library Catalogue No. 004811853. [British Library Catalogue -
http://explore.bl.uk/primo_library/libweb/action/search.do?dscnt=1&dstmp=1443853625
111&vid=BLVU1&fromLogin=true

16th Century

Burscough Priory. DDK/128/1-4, various dates, 1323 - 1590. [LRO]

The King to Sir William Pagett. DDK/5/1 28th May, 1 Edward VI., 1547. Grant of the site of the late Priory of Burscough....[LRO]

The King to Edward Earl of Derby. DDK/4/8 20th March, 28 Henry VIII., A.D. 1536-7. Contents: Copy Lease of the site and demesnes of Burscough Priory for 21 years. [LRO].

15th Century and earlier

Fonds Documents relating to Burscough Priory n.d. DDX 119. Notebook containing miscellaneous notes on Burscough Priory n.d. Transcript of Cartulary and Ancient Deeds of the Priory and also a photocopy of the original; transcripts of ancient deeds, (these transcripts are of the Burscough Register in TNA). Maps. Proceedings in witchcraft at Burscough priory 1454, (photocopy only). [LRO]

Ordination of Thomas Lytherland as subdeacon of Burscough Priory by John, Bishop of Coventry and Lichfield, at Eccleshall Church. DDIN 60/3 17 Mar. 1469/70 [LRO].

Chetham Society. Remains... 3rd series. Vol. 18, An edition of the cartulary of Burscough Priory / transcribed, edited and introduced by A. N. Webb. Manchester : C.S, 1970. 0719011523. [LCL]

An edition of the cartulary of Burscough Priory / [transcribed, edited and introduced by A. N. Webb]. Publisher A. N. Webb, 1966.
[LCL and online at http://books.google.com/books.]

Flixton, St Michael. Manchester Archives Department has acquittances by the prebendary of Flixton for the fruits of the church, 1369/70. (L1/19/1/1,2). A church existed at Flixton in the 12th century when it was granted to Burscough Priory. [Manchester Archives - http://www.manchester.gov.uk/info/448/archives_and_local_studies]

[Will of Thomas of Lathom] DDSC 43A/102 [1369.] Wishes to be buried in Burscough Priory; for prayers to be offered for him by the canons; and 40 shillings to the friars at Preston...etc [LRO]

Photographs of Duchy of Lancaster records: depositions DDX 2522/59 including a grant by Robert son of Richard Lord of Lathom, to Burscough Priory, of part of his land called Swinlehehurst in Anglezark, mid 13th cent (DL 25/645) [LRO]

Appendix 5

Penwortham Priory

Please see Appendix 1 - General Sources for full details of the main sources of information, and full references. The General Sources are not included below

21st Century
Lancashire Churches, by Tony Boughen. Includes Penwortham
[http://www.lancashirechurches.co.uk/index.htm]
Then and now. Lancashire Evening Post 19-Oct-2004 Page: 8 Cols: a-e Illustrated [LL]
Looking back. Lancashire Evening Post 24-Feb-2001 Page: 12 Cols c-e Illustrated [LL]
Ancient Priory could be building block to homes. Lancashire Evening Post 05-Jun-2000 Page: 7 Cols b-g Illustrated [LL]

20th Century
Council for British Archaeology Group 5: Archaeology north-west: the bulletin of CBA North West Vol 4 (Issue 14)/1999. 99/40. Four trial trenches - nothing found. LUAU. [LCL]
Atkinson, Andrew. The mad monk of Penwortham, and, Gentlemen of Penwortham Priory. 1998. Subject Penwortham Priory - Roger Norreis. [LCL]
Atkinson, Andrew. Penwortham Prior's alleged sex scandal - 500 years on the truth revealed : Henry VIII's plot closes Penwortham monastery : a true story. Subject Richard Hawkesbury. Penwortham : Author, 1998. [LCL]
Getting heads together. Lancashire Evening Post 21-Jul-1998 Page: 13 Cols a-g Illustrated [LL]
Discovery solves riddle of missing Priory stone. Lancashire Evening Post 29-Jun-1998 Page: 5 Cols b-g Illustrated [LL]
Riddle of Priory's stone treasures - missing 70yrs. Lancashire Evening Post 11-Jun-1998 Page: 11 Cols a-d [LL]
Mad monk's wicked ways. Lancashire Evening Post 15-Aug-1997 Page: 11 Cols b-h Illustrated [LL]
Blaess, Madeleine. 'Les manuscrits français dans les monastères anglais au Moyen Âge' [French manuscripts at English monasteries in the Middle Ages]. Romania, 94:3 (1973), 321-58. ISSN 0035-8029, [http://www.history.ac.uk/projects/bbih]
Turner, D. H. 'The Penwortham breviary'. British Museum Quarterly, 28:3-4 (1964), 85-8. [http://www.history.ac.uk/projects/bbih]
Penwortham Priory Relics to be preserved. Stone heads and heraldic stone signs. Preston Guardian 25-Sep-1926 Page: 9 Cols b-e Illustrated [LL]

History of the ancient Priory soon to be demolished. Preston Guardian 04-Jul-1925 Page: 9 Cols a-f Illustrated [LL]

Historic mansion dating from 1087 to be demolished after failing to be auctioned. Preston Guardian 27-Jun-1925 Page: 7 Col d [LL]

Photographs of Penwortham Priory taken by J.J. Pearson, shortly before the Priory was demolished P/91 [n.d.] [LRO]

Particulars and plan.... Uniform Title Penwortham Priory sale, 1925. Publisher Bridgnorth :"Journal", 1925. [LCL]

Catalogues for Sales by Auction of land etc. adjacent to the Ribble Navigation [no ref. or date] Penwortham Priory, 25 Jun.1925 DDPP 35/14 1925. Coloured plan. No history. [LRO]

The Times, Monday, Oct 06, 1924; pg. 24; col A. Priory for sale, includes picture. (Also The Times, Saturday, Jun 13, 1925; pg. 28; col A) [LCLDL]

The Times, Thursday, May 28, 1925; pg. 24; col E. Longer article about the Priory, about what will happen; for sale by auction. Demolition been avoided three times. [LCLDL]

Lancashire Image Archive: 3 images of Penwortham Priory before demolition, one during demolition, and two of Penwortham Priory Lodge (moved to Back Lane, Hutton in 1912) . [LL]

Penwortham Priory DDX 884/3-12 [n.d.] For photographs of this building, demolished in the 1920s, see P91. A plan of the property for sale in 1925 is at DDX 74/18/4. [LRO]

19th Century

Plan of Penwortham Priory, late 19th century. DDX 884. [LRO]

Penwortham. George Esdaile. Source: Lancashire and Cheshire Antiquarian Society Transactions Year: 1883 Volume (Issue): 1 Page: 46-52 Description: Includes information on Penwortham Priory [LL]

Photograph of Penwortham Church PR3164/14/27 1865/66. Photograph of Penwortham Church PR3164/14/28 1954 [LRO]

Photographs of Penwortham Priory PR3164/14/29 Undated 2 Items; PR3164/14/30 1863; PR3164/14/31 1901-1902 Photograph of painting of Lawrence Rawstorne, owner of Penwortham Priory PR3164/14/32 Early 19th cent [LRO]

The castle hill of Penwortham. Author: Thornber, Rev. William. Historic Society of Lancashire and Cheshire Volume: 9 (1856-1857) Pages: 61-76, illus. [LCL]

Local Intelligence. The Preston Chronicle etc (Preston, England), Thursday, Dec 24, 1857. Tunnel between Penwortham and Tulketh? [LCLDL]

A Peep at Penwortham and its Castle Hill. The Preston Chronicle etc (Preston, England), Saturday, November 29, 1856. [LCLDL]

Visit of the Lancashire & Cheshire Historic Society to Preston. The Preston Chronicle etc (Preston, England), Saturday, June 28, 1856. Full page report, includes excavations at Penwortham Castle, and mentions of Penwortham Priory. [LCLDL]

Penwortham Priory. The Preston Chronicle etc (Preston, England), Saturday, April 15, 1854. [LCLDL]

John Weld's sketch book DP 386/1 1830-1836 Contents: A book of pencil, ink and watercolour sketches by John Weld of Leagram Hall during the period c.1830-1886. Page: 42 Penwortham church. [LRO]

Miscellaneous plans and papers relating to Penwortham Priory. DDX 884 1850

- 1900 Deposited by Mr J Brandwood, Preston, 13 July 1973 (acc. 3147) [LRO]

17th Century
[Penwortham Priory] DDR 10/5 1375 - 1675. Contents: Extent of the Priory of Penwortham, 1375, with abstracts of other deeds. Covers up to May 1659. [LRO]

16th Century
Penwortham. DDR 10/11 7 Jul. 1564 Contents: Grant: for £660.17.6: Queen Elizabeth to John Fletewoode, esq. -- manor or grange of Penwortham and properties in Penwortham, Middelfourthe....etc....Henry VIII, 24 Jan. 1542/3 granted to J.F. reversion of site of priory...etc [LRO]

15th Century and earlier
The Henry Ogle Collection DDX 208 c14th century-1828. Scale drawings (many coloured) of glass, floor-tiles, churches, datestones, etc., including DDX 208/ 27-35 other glass Penwortham, St Mary's; DDX 208/46 Perpendicular doorway, Penwortham Parish Church DDX 208/84 Tower. Penwortham St Mary; DDX 208/93 Rubbings. 1653 Penwortham St Mary. [LRO]
Chetham Society. Remains... [1st series],Vol. 30 : Documents relating to the Priory of Penwortham and other possessions in Lancashire of the Abbey of Evesham, edited by W.A. Hulton. Publisher Manchester : C.S, 1853. [LCL]

Appendix 6

Preston Friars

Please see Appendix 1 - General Sources for full details of the main sources of information, and full references. The General Sources are not included below

21st Century
[Preston Friary excavations 2007 - miscellaneous items.] 4 coloured photos of excavations, including coffin etc., and burial. Full report not yet written up. Includes Report for site, but not including latest excavations. See also newspaper cuttings in Harris Library]. [LCL]

20th Century
Parkin, Wilfred. The Friars Preachers in Lancashire, 1260-1990. Excalibur, 1991. ISBN 185634097X. [LCL]
Records of HM Prison, Preston JAPR 1248-1974. Includes history of Preston's first House of Correction, former friary. [LRO]

19th Century
....Preston (Grey Friars). Baines Manuscript Collection. Handwritten copy of extract from Dugdale's Monasticon. BAI C 71 21. [LCL]

17th Century
Friary, Fryer Wind. [Preston] DDX/194/19 Undated. Shows Friars Wind (Fri-

argate) including Friary and lane leading to Friars Wind; also Lady Well. Prior to 1618 (or 1680?) when friary became House of Correction. [LRO]

16th Century
Ministers Accounts, Exchequer, relating to the property of the Grey Friars, Preston, and the Augustine Friars, Lancaster P/13 1539. PRO copy held in Lancashire Record Office; gloves recommended! In Latin. [LRO]

15th Century and earlier
[no title] DDPD 11/26 20 Jul. [1499]. Grant....to Philip Browne, D. Sac. Th. and Warden of the House of Friars Minor of the B.V.M. of Preston -- a parcel of common called Frere Lone......Given at Preston, 20 Jul. 14 Hen. VII. [LRO]

DDHK 9/1/3 1479/80. Contents: Preston Friary Indulgence, Issued to James Parker and Agnes his wife, with Hugh, Roger, George, Thomas and Elizabeth their children, by Brother James, warden of the minor friars of Preston. 27 Feb 1479/80. [LRO]

[Will of Thomas of Lathom] DDSC 43A/102 [1369.] ......also to the brothers of B. Augustine at Weryngton (Warrington) 5 marks. Also to the friars minor of Preston 40 shillings..... [LRO]

Appendix 7

Tulketh Abbey, Preston

Please see Appendix 1 - General Sources for full details of the main sources of information, and full references. The General Sources are not included below

20th Century
[Tulketh Hall - miscellaneous items]. LD41 TULKETH HALL. [LCL]
Tulketh Hall. Lancashire Evening Post: 25-Jan-1939 p. 6 [LL]

19th Century
Local Friaries and Priories. The Preston Chronicle etc (Preston, England), Saturday, February 14, 1891. [LCLDL]

Our Churches and Chapels. The Preston Chronicle etc (Preston, England), Saturday, November 13, 1869. Some suggest monks built Tulketh Hall, others that it existed prior to them. [LCLDL]

Tulketh Hall, near Preston... [sale catalogue]. Preston : Clarke (Printer), 1850. [LCL]

Lectures on the Antiquities and Topography of Preston. The Preston Chronicle etc (Preston, England), Saturday, November 3, 1849. [LCLDL]

A Legend of Tulketh Hall. The Preston Chronicle etc (Preston, England), Saturday, May 2, 1846. (Continued on 9th and 16th May). First paragraph a history including abbey. [LCLDL]

Appendix 8

Hospital of St Mary Magdalene, Preston

Please see Appendix 1 - General Sources for full details of the main sources of information, and full references. The General Sources are not included below

20th Century
St. Mary Magdalene's hospital, Preston. In Stray notes. Historic Society of Lancashire and Cheshire, Volume: 66 (1914) Pages: 274. 12 pages of cartulary in P.R.O., Carta Miscell., iii, 28. [LCL]

17th Century
[Lease] DX 1616 14 Feb. 1661/2. Lease..... a croft in the Maudelanes late belonging to the hospital of Mary Magdalen.... [LRO]

15th Century and earlier
Cartulary of the Hospital of St. Mary Magdalene, Preston P/70 Undated
Only dates given are: 29 Feb 1205/6, 22 Jul 1270, 23 June 1287 and 30 Jul 1313. [LRO]

Appendix 9

Fernyhalgh, Ladyewell Shrine

Please see Appendix 1 - General Sources for full details of the main sources of information, and full references. The General Sources are not included below

21st Century
St Mary's, Fernyhalgh and Ladyewell website; includes history.
www.ladyewellshrine.co.uk/
Thompson, Ian. The water of life : springs and wells of mainland Britain / by Ian and Frances Thompson. Cribyn : Llanerch, 2004. Contains a section on Ladyewell at Fernyhalgh. [LCL]

20th Century
Hundreds join Ladyewell pilgrimage. Lancashire Evening Post
10-Sep-1999 Page: 8 Cols efg [LL]
Ladyewell past and present. Preston : Newman College, [1998] [LCL]
Petition protest in bid to save historic route. Lancashire Evening Post 08-Oct-1996 Page 6 Cols b-g [LL]
Pilgrim's path set to take traffic. Lancashire Evening Post 02-Sept-1996 Page 9 Cols b-h [LL]
Having a shrine old time/Golden milestone - Fr.Ben. Lancashire Evening Post 21-Aug-1993 Pages 1 Cols efg, 13 Cols a-e- il [LL]
Swarbrick, Judith. The story of the old missionary altar, Ladyewell House, Fernyhalgh. No date. [LCL]
Warren, Leo. Fernyhalgh and its associations. Preston : Newman College Re-

sources Unit (Printer), 1990. [LCL]

Research papers concerning Burgess altar at Ladywell House, Fernyhaigh 1988 DDX 1782 [LRO]

Ripley, Francis. Our Lady's Lancashire shrine (St. Mary's, Fernyhalgh). Text of sermon preached at Fernyhalgh, August 15, 1965. [LCL]

Our Lady's Lancashire shrine (St. Mary's, Fernyhalgh). Preston : Primrose, [196]. [LCL]

Fernyhalgh. St Mary's R.C. Church. Book of remembrance (monumental inscriptions): St Mary's Chapel, Ladywell, Fernyhalgh / compiled by Jane Smyth. No date. Inscriptions in alphabetical order. - Includes a history of the Lady's Well and Chapel. [LCL]

St Mary's RC Church, Fernyhalgh RCFE 1681-1960 143. Files ...including..... Book containing "The traditional account of Our Lady's Well and Chapel in Fernyhalgh until 1685" and "A continuation of the Historical Account of the New Chappel House in Fernyhalgh" 1714-1723, both probably written by Christopher Tuttel, priest at Fernyhalgh RCFE 2/1 Undated [LRO]

Gillett, H. M. Our Lady's well at Fernyhalgh. Offprint from the "Catholic Fireside" Vol. 142, no. 3400. April 29, 1955. [LCL]

Our Lady of Fernyhalgh. Preston : T. Snape, 1954. History of Our Lady's Well (Spring) and the Fernyhalgh chapel. [LCL]

Ladywell Fernyhalgh. Preston : Snape (printer), 1946. [LCL]

Lancashire registers. 5, Fernyhalgh, Goosnargh and Alston Lane / edited by Richard L. Smith. Catholic Record Soc, Vol 31, 1932. [LCL]

19th Century

O'Hare, Daniel. An old Lancashire mission : being a brief history of the Church of Our Ladye of the Well at Fernyhalgh, near Preston. Reprinted from the "Ushaw magazine", December 1892. [LCL]

Bishop Goss at Fernyhalgh. The Preston Chronicle (Preston, England), Saturday, July 10, 1869; Issue 3028. [LCLDL]

Whittle, P.A. An account of St. Marie's Chapel at Fernyhalgh, in the township of Broughton,.. Preston : Printed by Henry Oakey, 1851. [LCL]

A Topographical Dictionary of England 1848 Author Samuel Lewis (editor) [http://www.british-history.ac.uk]

A Legend of "Our Lady's Well" at Fernyhalgh. The Preston Chronicle (Preston, England), Saturday, May 30, 1846. [LCLDL]

Appendix 10

Stydd Hospital and St Saviour's Chapel

Please see Appendix 1 - General Sources for full details of the main sources of information, and full references. The General Sources are not included below

21st Century

St Wilfrid's Ribchester, with St Saviour, Stydd. Includes history of St Saviour's, + times of worship etc. http://www.achurchnearyou.com/ribchester-stydd-st-saviour/

James Stanford and the Stanford Trust and Dole. Margaret Panikkar Lancashire History Quarterly 2008 Vol.12, issue 2, winter 2008 Pages 19-27. Illustrated. An account of the trust set up by the will of James Stanford which would provide a catholic priest for Stydd and Bailey and also poor relief for Ribchester, Stydd and Bailey. [LCL]

Lancashire Churches, by Tony Boughen. Includes Stydd, Ribchester etc, http://www.lancashirechurches.co.uk/stydd.htm,

Race against time to save historic churches Lancashire Evening Post 07-Jun-2004 Page: 8 [LL]

20th Century

A brief history of Stydd Church, [by] C.J. Ward [and others] 1986. History from 1292. Includes excavations in 1912/13, and 1971/72. [LCL]

Ribchester Parish St Wilfred: registers of marriages, services, and churchings, Dutton choir deeds and correspondence, PCC minutes, papers relating to Stidd, St Saviour, etc. 1756-1977. PR 3313 [LRO]

Kathleen Eyre of Lytham. Photographs DDEY/acc5582/36/5/31 Photographs: "The Real Lancashire" 8 Mar 1964 Almshouses of St John's Hospitalers of Jerusalem in Stydd. [LRO]

[Some local church histories.]. Includes A story of the parish church of St. Wilfred's, together with a brief account of St. Saviour's, Stydd...[LCL]

Illustrations relating to the history of Manchester and Salford and the surrounding district / prepared by a committee of the Manchester Branch of the Historical Association. Manchester : Sherratt & Hughes, 1932. Including Stydd Church. 29 cards held in folder. - For use in schools. - Includes illustrations from other parts of Lancashire and Cheshire. [LCL]

A story of the Parish Church of St. Wilfred's, Ribchester, together with a brief account of St Saviour's, Stydd. - 14th ed. Sidebotham, S. 1925 [LCL]

Ribchester Church and Stydd Chapel. Lancashire and Cheshire Antiquarian Society Transactions 1924. Volume (Issue): 41 Page: 40-3 [LL]

19th Century

Stydd Catholic Chapel Ribchester Reopening. Preston Guardian 12-Sep-1877 Page: 6 [LL]

Our Country Churches and Chapels. The Preston Chronicle, Saturday, December 3, 1870. By Atticus. Interesting contemporary description. [LCL]

The history of Stydd Chapel and Preceptory, near Ribchester, Lancashire : illus Latham, George. 1853. Includes many illustrations from around 1853. Gives history and detailed description. [LCL]

Plan PR3313/4/48 Undated. Plan, elevation and details of south side doorway of Stydd Chapel. Drawn and measured by George Latham. Approx. scale: - 1 in. to 3 ft. 26 x 17 cms., paper, ink. [LRO]

Plan PR3313/4/50 Undated. Plan of details for restoration in interior of Stydd Chapel Designed and drawn by George Latham Approx. scale: 1 in. to 3 ft. 26 x 17 cms., paper, ink. [LRO]

Plan PR3313/4/47 Undated Plan of Stydd Chapel, Ribchester Architects: Taylor and Young Scale: 1 in. to 8 ft. 39 x 28 cms., tracing paper, pencil. [LRO]

Proposed Renovation Of Stydd Church. The Preston Chronicle (Preston, England), Saturday, February 24, 1849. [LCLDL]

Hospital at Langrigh: grant of charter by Alan de Singleton. Baines Manuscript Collection. Hospital of St. Saviour - Stidd Under Longridge - Stydd - Sted. Handwritten copy of extract from Dugdale [Monasticon?], vol. 7. Relates to the Hospital of St. Saviour at Stidd Under Longridge which was granted land by Alan de Singleton. [LCL]

John Weld's sketch book DP 386/1 1830-1836. A book of pencil, ink and water-colour sketches by John Weld of Leagram Hall during the period c.1830-1886. Includes: Page: 1 description: Stidd chapel; Page: 2 description: Stidd tombstone and font. [LRO]

Sketch-books of William Latham [no ref.] 1809 - 1823. Stydd Chapel DP 291/58 31 Oct. 1822 Font, Stydd Chapel DP 291/59 31 Oct. 1822 p. 58. Stydd from South, showing growth on east end of roof. 1822. p 59 - font. [LRO]

18th Century

Disbursements of Dob Hall Dole in Ribchester and at Stidd. Almhouses PR2905/5/1 1792-1807 [LRO]

15th Century and earlier

The Henry Ogle Collection DDX 208 c14th century-1828. Scale drawings (many coloured) of glass, floor-tiles, churches, datestones, etc., including DDX 208/41 Norman doorway, Stydd; DDX 208/41 Transitional, Stydd. Also several of St Wilfred's, Ribchester. [LRO]

Appendix 11

Whalley Abbey

Please see Appendix 1 - General Sources for full details of the main sources of information, and full references. The General Sources are not included below

21st Century

Whalley Abbey website. Includes history, etc.
[http://www.whalleyabbey.co.uk/]

Whalley Abbey Gatehouse, English Heritage. [http://www.english-heritage.org.uk/visit/places/whalley-abbey-gatehouse/]

Scheduled Ancient Monument - Whalley Abbey. Brief history and description of remains. [http://www.lancashire.gov.uk/corporate/web/view.asp?siteid=4398&pageid=20451&e=e:]

Lancashire Churches, by Tony Boughen. Includes Whalley etc, http://www.lancashirechurches.co.uk/stydd.htm,

Cistercians in Yorkshire Project, but information on other Cistercian houses too, including Furness, Sawley and Whalley.
[http://cistercians.shef.ac.uk/abbeys/furness.php]

The Conference Centre, Whalley Abbey, Whalley, Lancashire : tree-ring analysis of timbers; Martin Bridge. (Research Department report series (English Heritage. Research Dept.), 66/2007). [England]: English Heritage, 2007. 16 p.2 [http://www.history.ac.uk/projects/bbih]

Snape, Michael Francis. 'The Church in a Lancashire parish : Whalley, 1689-1800'.

In Gregory, Jeremy; Chamberlain, Jeffrey S. (ed.), The national church in local perspective : the Church of England and the regions, 1660-1800 (Studies in modern British religious history, 5) (Woodbridge: Boydell, 2003), 243-64. ISBN 0851158978.4 [http://www.history.ac.uk/projects/bbih]

Snape, Michael Francis. The Church of England in industrialising society : the Lancashire parish of Whalley in the eighteenth century (Studies in modern British religious history, 9). Woodbridge; Rochester (NY): Boydell, 2003. xii, 228 p. ISBN 1843830140.5 [http://www.history.ac.uk/projects/bbih]

Mullett, Michael A. 'The Reformation in the parish of Whalley'. In Poole, Robert (ed.), The Lancashire witches : histories and stories (Manchester: Manchester University Press, 2002), 88-104. ISBN 0719062047.7
[http://www.history.ac.uk/projects/bbih]

Snape, Michael Francis. 'Poverty and the northern clergy in the eighteenth century : the parish of Whalley, 1689-1789'. Northern History, 36 (2000), 83-98. Publisher: Maney. ISSN 0078172X.8 [http://www.history.ac.uk/projects/bbih]

Duckworth, Catherine. 'With injustice and oppression I make no compromise : the Easter dues question'. In Halstead, Susan; Duckworth, Catherine (ed.), Aspects of Accrington : discovering local history (Barnsley: Wharncliffe, 2000), 100-11. ISBN 1871647657,
[http://www.history.ac.uk/projects/bbih]

20th Century

The book of hours of Braddyll family of Whalley. Historic Society of Lancashire and Cheshire Trans 1997 Volume (Issue): 146 Pages 1-30 [LL]

Whalley and District Historical and Archaeological Society. Where rivers meet. Vol. 6, No. 2, January, 1995: Whalley Abbey gatehouses architectural discoveries / by John S. Chadwick and Milton B. Ormerod. Whalley & District Historical & Archaeological Soc, 1995. Issue devoted to Whalley Abbey. [LCL]

Opus Anglicanum and renaissance velvet : the Whalley Abbey vestments / Monnas, Lisa. 1994 [http://www.history.ac.uk/projects/bbih]

Aston, Michael. Monasteries. Series Know the landscape. London : Batsford, 1993. ISBN 0713467096 Includes references to Salley (Sawley) Abbey, Tulketh and Whalley Abbey. [LCL]

King, C. D. The Whalley Coucher book and the dialectal phonology of Lancashire and Cheshire, 1175-1350. Subject Whalley Abbey. Thesis (Ph.D), University of St. Andrews, 1991. [LCL]

Was St Tuda buried at Whalley? / Lewis, Christopher Piers. HSLC vol 138. pp 221-224. 1989,
[http://www.hslc.org.uk/index_search.php?section=23&type=index]

Opit, Judith L. Whalley Abbey. Publisher Burnley Curriculum Development Centre, 1982. [LCL]

Closing scenes in the history of Whalley Abbey and its Abbot.
Burnley Express 12-Jan-1971 Page: 6, Cols a-i [LL]

Whalley Abbey and the last of its Abbots.
Burnley Express 05-Jan-1971 Page: 6 [LL]

Ashmore, Owen. A guide to Whalley Abbey. Edition 3rd ed. Publisher Blackburn Diocesan Board of Finance, 1968. [LCL]

John Paslew, last abbot of Whalley / Whalley, Gwilym. 1967,

[http://www.history.ac.uk/projects/bbih]

Newsletter, Whalley Abbey Today PR3076/14/23, 1964, Nov, 1965, Mar. [LRO]

The Whalley Abbey bursars' account for 1520 Historic Society of Lancashire and Cheshire Trans 1962 Volume (Issue): 114, Page: 59-72 [LL]

The varied fortunes of Whalley Abbey. Burnley Express 13-Mar-1954 Page: 9 [LL]

Wallis, John Eyre Winstanley. Whalley Abbey : a short sketch of its history and buildings / with a preface by the Lord Bishop of Blackburn. Edition 4th ed. Publisher S.P.C.K, 1947. Photocopy. [LCL]

Haworth, Chas. The Abbot of Whalley, or Paslew's last penance. Series Legends and Stories of Lancashire; No. 2 Blackburn : Haworth & Johnson, [No date] Subject John Paslew - Whalley Abbey. A fictional account of the last days of John Paslew. [LCL]

Lambert, Charles Henry. Whalley Abbey : yesterday and to-day. Edition 6th ed. Publisher Blackburn : Provincial Newspapers Ltd, 1955. [LCL]

Knowles, David. Monastic sites from the air, by David Knowles and J.K.S. St Joseph. C.U.P, 1952. Interesting photos; only covers Furness, Cockersand, Sawley, Whalley from Lancashire. [LCL]

An ancient vestment Burnley Express 04-Nov-1950 [LL]

Lambert, Charles Henry. Whalley Abbey : yesterday and to-day. 2nd ed. Publisher Blackburn : Provincial Newspapers Ltd, 1949. [LCL]

Monks celebrate mass at Whalley Abbey after 400 years Preston Guardian 22-May-1937 Page: 9 [LL]

Order of service of re-dedication of Whalley Abbey DDX 1936/7/4 1936 14 Jun [LRO]

McNulty, Joseph B. Whalley Abbey : its beginning and end. Clitheroe : Advertiser & Times (Printers), [19] [LCL]

Whalley Abbey. [Photograph album]. Publisher Hove : Marshall, Keene, [1935]. Cover title.- 7 black & white photographs in album. [LCL]

Tile memorial and other medieval tiles at Whalley. Lancashire and Cheshire Antiquarian Society Transactions 1933 Volume 49, pp 95-103 [LL]

Illustrations relating to the history of Manchester and Salford and the surrounding district / prepared by a committee of the Manchester Branch of the Historical Association. Manchester : Sherratt & Hughes, 1932. Includes Whalley Abbey... 29 cards held in folder. - For use in schools. - Includes illustrations from other parts of Lancashire and Cheshire. [LCL]

Wallis, John Eyre Winstanley. The narrative of the indictment of the traitors of Whalley and Cartmell, 1536-7. Publisher Manchester : Chetham Soc, 1931. Reprinted from "Remains Historical and Literary..." of Chetham Society, new series, vol. 90, 1931. [LCL]

The Times, Monday, Mar 26, 1928; pg. 19; Issue 44851; col D. Whalley Abbey. A Great Cistercian House   [LCLDL]

The Times, Monday, Mar 26, 1928; pg. 20; col A. Whalley Abbey: A Cistercian House In Lancashire. Includes 2 pictures. [LCLDL]

McNulty, Joseph B. The last days of Sawley and Whalley abbeys, (1536-1537). Clitheroe Advertiser & Times (Printers), [1926?] [LCL]

Wallis, John Eyre Winstanley. Whalley Abbey : a short sketch of its history and buildings. Edition 2nd ed. Publisher Manchester, SPCK, 1924. [LCL]

The Times, Wednesday, Jul 30, 1924; pg. 15; Issue 43717; col E. Whalley Abbey: The Last House Of The White Monks. [LCLDL]

Wallis, John Eyre Winstanley. Whalley Abbey : a short sketch of its history and buildings, [and], The history of the Church in Clitheroe, 1122-1922. Publisher SPCK, 1923. [LCL]

Purchase of Abbey by Manchester Diocesan Board Preston Guardian 24-Nov-1923 Page: 3 [LL]

The Times, Monday, Jul 23, 1923; pg. 13; Issue 43400; col F Whalley Abbey. W. Manchester. Letter to the editor. [LCLDL]

Pilgrimage to the Abbey on the 200th Anniversary of the execution of John Paslew, the last abbot. Preston Guardian 17-Mar-1923 Page: 17, Cols d-f [LL]

Whalley Abbey was purchased by the Church of England. Preston Guardian 25-Nov-1922 Page: 6, Col a-b [LL]

The Times, Saturday, Nov 18, 1922; pg. 7; col D. Wholly Abbey Sold. Cistercian Buildings For Church Of England. [LCLDL]

15th century vestment at Towneley Hall Burnley News 08-Jul-1922 Page: 5, Cols a-d [LL]

The selling at Sothebys of some of the vestments taken from Whalley Abbey at the time of the dissolution of the monasteries. Preston Guardian 17-Jun-1922 Page: 14, Col b-e [LL]

Roman Catholic Church Whalley The purchase of part of the Abbey Farm to be converted into a church. Preston Guardian 25-Feb-1922 Page: 12 [LL]

Note on the bells at Downham. Lancashire and Cheshire Antiquarian Society Transactions 1920 Volume (Issue): 38 Page: 138-46 [LL]

Some fifteenth century carvings from Whalley Abbey. Historic Society of Lancashire and Cheshire Transactions 1914 Volume 66, pp. 272-3 [LL]

Whalley: Whalley Abbey, abbot's lodgings DDX 1572/1/34 1907 [LRO]

Great Britain. Royal Commission on Historical Manuscripts. Report on manuscripts in various collections. Vol. 2, The manuscripts of Sir George Wombwell, the Duke of Norfolk, Lord Edmund Talbot, Miss Buxton, Mrs Harford and Mrs Wentworth of Woolley. Series Cd; 932 Publisher HMSO, 1903. Subject Whalley Abbey Duchy of Lancaster Robert Pylkington Stanley. [LCL]

Roper, William Oliver. Lancaster and English history : read before the Philosophical Society of Lancaster. Subjects include Whalley Abbey. [LCL]

Act book of the ecclesiastical court of Whalley, 1510-38 / Cooke, Alice Margaret, 1867-1940. 1901 [http://www.history.ac.uk/projects/bbih]

19th Century

Inventory of the Goods of Whalley Abbey, Lancashire, 1537. Reliquary 7, Jan 1893, p 34-38. [British Periodicals Collection, UMI]

Assheton, Ralph. The abbey lands of Whalley, in the county of Lancaster. Publisher Mitchell & Hughes, 1887. After Dissolution. Braddyl and Assheton families etc. [LCL]

Whalley Church and Abbey visit Lancashire and Cheshire Antiquarian Society Transactions 1885 Volume 3, pp. 227-33 [LL]

Johnson, Thomas. A pictorial handbook to the valley of the Ribble being a complete guide to the tourist or the stranger visiting Blackburn, Wilpshire, Ribchester, Whalley, Mitton, Stoneyhurst, Clitheroe, Pendle Hill, Sawley Abbey, Gisburn, Gordale Scar & Malham Cove. Edition [Rev. ed.] 1882.

Blackburn : Haworth & Johnson. Rev. ed. of "From Blackburn to Gisburn: a handbook for tourists and travellers". [LCL]

Whalley Abbey, near Blackburn, Lancashire, and, Blackburn Cathedral / [by] G.A. Williams. Bound "tete-beche". No date. [LCL]

[Photographs taken by Grant family of Burnley, c.1880-83.]. Subjects include Whalley Abbey. Contains photos in sepia on Whalley Abbey, etc [LCL]

Waddington, William A. Cistercian architecture, as illustrated. The remains of Whalley abbey. Volume: 26 (1873-1874) Pages: 145-162, illus., plan, [http://www.hslc.org.uk/index_search.php?section=23&type=index]

Whitaker, Thomas Dunham. An history of the original parish of Whalley, and honor of Clitheroe...Vol.1. 4th ed. / revised and enlarged by John Gough Nichols and Ponsonby A. Lyons. 1872.+ Vol 2. [LCL]

Mannex and Co. Directory of North and East Lancashire, &c. with historical sketches of Furness and Whalley Abbeys and the religious orders; and an original essay on the geology of the Lake District, &c... Preston : P. Mannex, 1868. [LCL]

Inventory of Whalley Abbey Historic Society of Lancashire and Cheshire Transactions 1867 Volume 19, pp. 103-10 [LL]

The Coucher Book, or Chartulary of Whalley Abbey. Athenaeum 1091, 23 Sept 1848, p 955-6. [British Periodicals Collection, UMI]

Whalley Abbey. Preston Chronicle (Preston, England), Saturday, May 21, 1842; Issue 1551. History and description. [LCLDL]

A visit to Whalley Abbey and Pendle Hill, Preston Chronicle Saturday, September 14, 1839; Issue 1411. Description of remains as at 1839. [LCLDL]

John Weld's sketch book DP 386/1 1830-1836. A book of pencil, ink and watercolour sketches by John Weld of Leagram Hall during the period c.1830-1886. The subjects include: Page: 4: Whalley Abbey; Page: 5 Whalley Abbey; Page: 6 Whalley crosses and tombstones; Page: 7 Whalley Abbey;
Page: 45 Whalley church interior; Page: 49 Furness effigies. Whalley brass; Page: 51 Whalley. Chorley. Ribchester. [LRO]

Sketch-books of William Latham [no ref.] 1809 - 1823. Includes: Whalley Abbey DP 291/60 Undated; Whalley Churchyard Cross DP 291/61 31 Oct. 1822; Whalley Churchyard Cross DP 291/62 31 Oct. 1822 [LRO]

MOULDINGS [no ref. or date] drawings of Whalley Abbey DDX208/70 Undated [LRO]

Masonry Arch respond. Whalley Abbey DDX208/55 Undated (drawings). [LRO]

18th Century
DP 189 Buck's views of ... Whalley abbey 1727-1728 Nathaniel Buck. [LRO]

17th Century
Volume containing copies of evidences of title relating to Whalley Abbey and Sawley Abbey, 596-1368 DDB 85/7 1627 [LRO]
16th Century
Grant by letters patent of Henry VIII to John Braddyll of Whalley for £220.10s DP 355/2 16 Jul. 1546 [LRO]

Grant by letters patent of Henry VIII to John Braddyll of Whalley for £393.12s.6d DP 355/1 23 Mar. 1544/5 [LRO]

Whalley Abbey survey, 1537. [LCL]

Life, love, and death in north-east Lancashire, 1510 to 1537 : a translation of the Act Book of the Ecclesiastical Court of Whalley; edited by members of the Ranulf Higden Society led by Margaret Lynch ; general editor, P.H.W. Booth. (Chetham Society, Remains ... connected with the Palatine counties of Lancaster and Chester, 3rd ser., 46). Manchester: Chetham Society, 2006. ix, 283 p. ISBN 9780955427602; 0955427606.3, [http://www.history.ac.uk/projects/bbih]

15th Century and earlier

Letters Patent of Edward IV settling the dispute between the Abbey of Whalley and Christopher Parsons, rector of Slaytbourn, over the tithes of Halflat in Bowland. Duchy of Lancaster seal DDBR 19/9 27 May, 1482 [LRO]

Charters of the Borough of Clithoroe PR5013/1/9 1409 6 Dec. Language: English and Latin. Contents: 1 Henry IV 2 The Sheriff of Lancashire Letters patent from 1 to 2 ordering the proclamation at Whalley and elsewhere of the dissolution of the fairs customarily held, without authority, in the precincts of the Abbey at Whalley on the feasts of the Conception and Assumption of the blessed Virgin Mary, and recording the grant of two fairs to Clitheroe [LRO]

Confirmation of the grant to Stanlaw Abbey of the advowson of Whalley and of the chapels DDBR 19/8 20 Oct. 1399. [LRO]

Whalley Abbey : transcriptions of documents relating to Whalley. Typescript transcribed by Walter Bennett. [LCL]

Chetham Society. Remains... [1st series], Vols. 10, 11, 16 and 20 : The coucher book or chartulary of Whalley Abbey / edited by W.A. Hulton. Publisher Manchester : C.S, 1847. Vol 10 has a Contents list in English for all four volumes. Text in Latin. Vol 20 has an Appendix in English listing the demesne lands of Whalley just after the Dissolution (pp 1184-1254) and an Inventory of the Abbey by the Commissioners dated 24 March 1537 (pp 1255-1265). [LCL]

The Henry Ogle Collection DDX 208 c14th century-1828 Scale drawings (many coloured) of glass, floor-tiles, churches, datestones, etc., including DDX 208/ 40 Floor tiles Whalley Abbey Chapter House, 2 tiles; DDX 208/55   Masonry. Arch respond. Whalley Abbey;   DDX 208/56   Base. Whalley Abbey; DDX 208/70 Mouldings, full scale. Whalley Abbey;   DDX 208/57   Capital. Whalley Abbey [LRO]

Confirmation by the Prior of Coventry of the charter of the ordination of the vicarage of Whalley, granted 21 Mar. 1330/1 by Roger, Bishop of Coventry and Lichfield. Seal DDBR 19/3 21 May, 1331. [LRO]

Agreement DDM 34/7 3 Jun. 1328 The Abbey of Whalley and Sir Richard of Hoghton -- concerning the mill on the Alt at Ravensmeols. (Printed in Coucher Book of Whalley, Chet Soc. 515). [LRO]

Licence of Edward II for Thomas, Earl of Lancaster, to grant to Whalley Abbey a moiety of the manor of Bilyngton. SEAL DDBR 19/2 10 Nov. 1318. Related information: See Coucher Book of Whalley, p.938. [LRO]

Confirmation by Edward II of the grant made by Thomas, Earl of Lancaster, 25 July, 1316, to Whalley Abbey, of Tocstath and Smethedon. Seal fragment DDBR 19/1 23 Nov. 1316. Related information: See Coucher Book of Whalley, p.530. [LRO]

Appendix 12

Sawley Abbey

Please see Appendix 1 - General Sources for full details of the main sources of information, and full references. The General Sources are not included below

21st Century
Cistercians in Yorkshire Project, but information on other Cistercian houses too, including Furness, Sawley and Whalley.
[http://cistercians.shef.ac.uk/index.php]

Sawley Abbey, English Heritage: [http://www.english-heritage.org.uk/visit/places/sawley-abbey/]

Sawley Abbey, Sawley, Lancashire : a Cistercian monastic precinct and post-medieval landscape : survey report / Abby Hunt [and others]. Archaeological investigation report series; A1/17/2005. NMR, English Heritage, 2005. Illustrated. Survey Jul-Sept 2004. Detailed history and description of developments in the building. Good bibliography. Large scale map showing whole abbey precinct. [LCL]

Sawley in North Yorkshire; Lilian Chandler. Dallowgill: The author, 2005. [http://www.history.ac.uk/projects/bbih]

Jamroziak, Emilia M. 'Making and breaking the bonds : Yorkshire Cistercians and their neighbours'. In Kinder, Terryl N. (ed.), Perspectives for an architecture of solitude : essays on Cistercians, art and architecture in honour of Peter Fergusson (Medieval church studies, 11; Cîteaux. Studia et documenta, 13) (Turnhout: Brepols, 2004), 63-70. ISBN 2503516920; 9080543950.
[http://www.history.ac.uk/projects/bbih]

Coppack, Glyn; Hayfield, Colin. 'Sawley Abbey : the architecture and archaeology of a smaller Cistercian abbey'. Journal of the British Archaeological Association, 155 (2002), 22-114. Publisher: British Archaeological Association. ISSN 00681288. ISSN (electronic) 17476704.6,
[http://www.history.ac.uk/projects/bbih]

Coppack, Glyn. 'The Planning of Cistercian Monasteries in the Later Middle Ages : the Evidence from Fountains, Rievaulx, Sawley and Rushen'. In Clark, James G. (ed.), The religious orders in pre-Reformation England (Studies in the history of medieval religion, 18) (Woodbridge: Boydell, 2002), 197-209. ISBN 0851159001. [http://www.history.ac.uk/projects/bbih]

Cassidy-Welch, Megan. Monastic spaces and their meanings : thirteenth-century English Cistercian monasteries (Medieval church studies, 1). Turnhout: Brepols, 2001. xv, 293 p. ISBN 2503510892.8,
[http://www.history.ac.uk/projects/bbih]

20th Century
Sawley Abbey : a celebration of 850 years. Publisher Heritage Trust for North West, [1997]. [LCL]

Harvey, P.D.A. The Sawley Map and other World Maps in Twelfth-Century England. Imago Mundi Vol 49, 1997, p 33-42. [JSTOR]

Aston, Michael. Monasteries. Series Know the landscape. Publisher London :

Batsford, 1993. ISBN 0713467096 [LCL]

The Sixteenth-Century History of Two Cambridge Books from Sawley. Transactions of the Cambridge Bibliographical Society Vol 7:4, 1980, p 427-444. (EBSCOHost]

Dumville, David N. 'Celtic-Latin Texts in Northern England, c.1150-c.1250'. Celtica, 12 (1977), 19-49. ISSN 0069-1399,
[http://www.history.ac.uk/projects/bbih]

Farmer, Hugh. 'Stephen of Sawley'. The Month, ns, 29:6 (1963), 332-42. [http://www.history.ac.uk/projects/bbih]

Sawley Abbey. Burnley Express 14-Aug-1954 Page: 8 Cols d-g. Illus. Abbey that was founded a century before that at Whalley - Sawley Abbey. [LL]

Clay, Charles Travis, Sir, 1885-1978. 'The early abbots of the Yorkshire Cistercian houses'. Yorkshire Archaeological Journal, 38:149 (1952), 8-43. Publisher: Maney. ISSN 00844276. [http://www.history.ac.uk/projects/bbih]

Knowles, David. Monastic sites from the air, by David Knowles and J.K.S. St Joseph. C.U.P, 1952. Interesting photos; only covers Furness, Cockersand, Sawley, Whalley from Lancs. [LCL]

Halstead, Gerald. Sawley Abbey, Yorks. : a survey of the remains. Clitheroe : Author, [1951]. [LCL]

Cowles, Frederick. 'The eighth centenary of a Yorkshire abbey'. The Month, 185:968 (1948), 182-4. [http://www.history.ac.uk/projects/bbih]

Research papers of Fr Joseph McNulty. Abbeys of Whalley and Sawley DDX 732/1/5 Illustrations/Papers. No date. Printed Illustrations and Plans of Sawley Abbey. Copy transcription of "The Castle of Love" by a Monk of Sawley "Sallay Abbey (1148-1536)" by Joseph McNulty (1940). [LRO]

Sawley Abbey Estate near Clitheroe on the Borders of Lancashire and the West Riding of Yorkshire. SB00013 14 May 1935. Sale particulars. [EHNMR]

Sawley Abbey Estate DDX 2096/1 14 May 1935. [LRO]

An Old Bequest. Sawley Abbey Sold (Property) The Times Wednesday, May 15, 1935; pg. 10; Issue 47064. Estate sold to Mr Fattorini of Bradford for £80,000 [LCLDL]

Hampton & Sons, (Property) The Times Wednesday, May 09, 1934; pg. 30; Issue 46749 Sawley Abbey estate for sale again. [LCLDL]

MCNULTY, Joseph B. The last days of Sawley and Whalley abbeys, (1536-1537). Publisher Clitheroe Advertiser & Times (Printers), [1926?] [LCL]

Harrods, Ltd., London, S.W.1. (Property) The Times Tuesday, Feb 19, 1924; pg. 22; Issue 43579 Sale by auction, includes Sawley Abbey. [LCLDL]

Johnson, Thomas. A pictorial handbook to the valley of the Ribble : being a complete guide to the tourist or the stranger visiting Wilpshire, Ribchester, Langho, Whalley, Mitton, Stoneyhurst, Clitheroe, Pendle Hill, Sawley Abbey.... and the source of the Ribble. 6th ed. Blackburn : Author (Printer), 1911. [LCL]

Etchings By Sir Seymour Haden. (News) The Times Friday, May 06, 1910; pg. 6; [Includes one of Sawley Abbey] [LCLDL]

19th Century

Salley Abbey and Clitheroe Castle. British Architect 6:6, 11 Aug 1876, p 83-4. [British Periodicals Collection, UMI]

Ramble by the Ribble. The Preston Chronicle, Saturday, August 11, 1860; Issue 2495. Salley Abbey [LCLDL]

Historical account of the Cistercian Abbey of Salley in Craven, Yorkshire, founded A.D. 1147 : its foundation and benefactors, abbots, possessions, compotus and dissolution and its existing remains / edited by J. Harland. Publisher London : Clitheroe : Russell Smith ; Whewell, 1853. [LCL]

Excavations at Fountains Abbey.-Earl de (News) The Times Saturday, May 07, 1853; pg. 7 col F. Sawley Abbey 'a great rubbish heap', re excavations. [LCLDL]

Papers relating to Samuel James Allen and Family. Sketches of Sawley (Salley) Abbey, Yorkshire. Acc 100/SO1/131-150, 1850s. [York City Archives Department]

Researches at Salley Abbey. The Preston Chronicle, Saturday, May 26, 1849. [LCLDL]

Engraving by Basire showing view of the remains of Salley Abbey AL0130/049/01 01 Dec 1804. [EHNMR]

18th Century

Engraving by Sparrow showing view of the remains of Salley Abbey AL0130/049/02 07 Jan 1787 [EHNMR]

Henry Guy of Sawley Abbey. co. York QJB/10/53 June 1725 [LRO]

17th Century

Volume containing copies of evidences of title relating to Whalley Abbey and Sawley Abbey, 596-1368 DDB 85/7 1627. [LRO]

Kenyon of Peel Historical Manuscripts Commission 14th Report, Appendix PI IV (1894) `The Manuscripts of Lord Kenyon'. DDKE/HMC/42a Letter from: R[alph] A[sheton] to Mr. Johnson - Salley.--Complaining of Lord Haye's agent. Mr. Richmond, who will not permit him "so much as take a stone out of the old decaied Abbey walls to buyld or repaire" upon his lands at Salley. Date 8 Oct 1618. [LRO]

Memorandum E7/27/4/8 n.d. after 1605. Concerning Holme Knott's status as part of the manor of Sawley, and extracts from court rolls and the accounts of The Abbey of Sawley. [Greater Manchester County Record Office]

16th Century

Crown confirmation of grant of manors and lands in Yorkshire and Lancashire MD335/6/68/1 9 May 1538 Confirmation by Henry VIII to Sir Arthur D'arcy, knight, of manors, lands and rents including the site of Sawley Abbey with all demesne lands......[Bradfer-Lawrence, Harry, 1887-1965, land agent and antiquary]

15th Century and earlier

SAWLEY Abbey: miscellaneous typescript transcripts and plan. [LCL]

Yorkshire Archaeological Society. Record series. Vol. 87, for the year 1933, The chartulary of the Cistercian abbey of St. Mary of Salley in Craven. Vol. 1 (nos. 1-388) / transcribed and edited by Joseph McNulty. Y.A.S, 1933. Subject Sawley Abbey. Completed after 1333. 676 deeds (1-388 in Vol 1). Mostly about land possessed in Yorks and Lancs. [LCL]

Yorkshire Archaeological Society. Record series. Vol. 90, for the year 1934, The chartulary of the Cistercian abbey of St. Mary of Salley in Craven. Vol. 2 / transcribed and edited by Joseph McNulty. Publisher Y.A.S, 1934. Subject Sawley Abbey. List of abbots. Sallay Compotus of 1481 - not text. [LCL]

Sawley in Bowland, charters 12th century-16th century (copy) MS 382 [19th century-20th century]. [Yorkshire Archaeological Society]

Religious Houses, Deeds MD335/7 12th century-16th century 31 items
Deeds relating to the estates and interests of religious houses: 1.... 10: Cockersand Abbey....12: Hospitallers.....18-27: Sawley Abbey. [Bradfer-Lawrence, Harry, 1887-1965, land agent and antiquary]

Abbeys of Sawley and Furness. SAL/MS/615 4 Apr. 1329
Agreement between the abbots and convents of Sawley, Yorks., and Furness, Lancs., about the tithes of the manor of Winterbourne, in Gargrave, Yorks. [Society of Antiquaries of London]

Gargrave: documents relating to disputes over the payment of tithes DD130 18th century-19th century. Includes translation of the appropriation of Gargrave church to the abbey of Sawley, from the register of Archbishop William Melton [1321] [Yorkshire Archaeological Society]

Copy grant of market and fair. MD335/7/26 ?16th century. Related information: MD335/7/25 is original grant. Copy of royal grant of market and fair to Sawley Abbey, 1260 [Former ref: Monastic Houses. Box 65/26] [Bradfer-Lawrence, Harry, 1887-1965, land agent and antiquary]

Appendix 13

Cockerham Priory

Please see Appendix 1 - General Sources for full details of the main sources of information, and full references. The General Sources are not included below

21st Century

Personal communication. Owner/farmer of Cockerham Hall farm: this Hall was the site of the priory. Monks may have built flood bank; had water mill below priory, and windmill above (Mill Cottage on Mill Hill behind, plus Old Mill House by the road).

Marshall, Brian. Cockersand Abbey : a Lancashire house of Premonstratensian canons, 1180-1539. Publisher Landy Publishing, 2001. Includes information about Cockerham Priory. [LCL]

20th Century

Two custumals of the manor of Cockerham. Lancashire and Cheshire Antiquarian Society Transactions 1954, Volume 64, pp. 38-54. Custumals (customs of manor) dated 1326 and 1483. [LCL]

15th Century and earlier

Leicester Abbey cartulary (Cockerham part). Cockersand Abbey. MS LAUD, MISC, 625. Difficult to decipher Latin!. 15 pages; mainly rentals? [LCL]

Files containing Typescript and Manuscript. News Cuttings and Photocopies ZMM/1-29 [n.d.] Including Cockerham Priory, Bolton Charter 1253 & Richard III ZMM/3 No date [Bolton Archive and Local Studies Service]

Appendix 14

Cockersand Abbey

Please see Appendix 1 - General Sources for full details of the main sources of information, and full references. The General Sources are not included below

21st Century

Premonstratensians' website. Includes many references. [http://www.premontre.org/chapter/index.php]

Burn, Andrew et al. Cockersand Abbey, Thurnham, Lancashire: an analytical earthwork study. English Heritage Research Department Report No 55-2009, 2009. ISSN 1749-8775. [http://services.english-heritage.org.uk/ResearchReportsPdfs/055-2009WEB.pdf]

Marshall, Brian. Cockersand Abbey : a Lancashire house of Premonstratensian canons, 1180-1539. Landy Publishing, 2001. [LCL]

20th Century

Higham, Mary C. 'Place-names and past landscapes : the evidence from monastic charters'. In Nicolaisen, Wilhelm Fritz Hermann (ed.), Proceedings of the XIXth International Congress of Onomastic Sciences, Aberdeen, August 4-11, 1996. 3 vols. (University of Aberdeen, Department of English, 1998), Vol. 2, 178-85. ISBN 1-902355-00-8. [http://www.history.ac.uk/projects/bbih]

White, Andrew. 'Setting the scene, 1193-1500' [Lancaster]. In: White, Andrew, 1948- (ed.), A history of Lancaster, 1193-1993 (Keele: Ryburn, 1993), 9-48. [http://www.history.ac.uk/projects/bbih]

Spalding, John R. Cockersands Abbey. Publisher Author, [1989] Duplicated typescript. [LCL]

Papers of Ben Edwards, former County Archaeologist Archaeology files. DDX 541/acc10213/13. 20th cent. Papers, drawings, photographs and copy documents re-Cockersand Well and Cockersand Abbey, 1924-1986. [LRO]

Floods at Cockersand Abbey. Lancaster Guardian 18 February 1983 Page Nos:16 Illustrated. Floods at Cockersand Abbey reveal an underground passage, which may be a drain. [LL]

Sherdley, H.; White, A. J. 'Excavations at Cockersand abbey, Lancashire 1923-27'. Contrebis: a bulletin of archaeology for Lancashire and the North-West, 3:1 (1975), 1-18. Publisher: Lancaster Archaeological Society. ISSN 0307-5087. History, Info from Cartulary (see Chetham Soc). p. 4 Plan of Abbey, based on Excavation Committee plan of 1923-4. p. 6 Plan of Pilling Old Church, excavated 1924, and 1952. p. 10 Summary of sequence of building. Drawings and description of tiles, pottery, and metalwork. [LCL]

Knowles, David. Monastic sites from the air, by David Knowles and J.K.S. St Joseph. C.U.P, 1952. Search Room. H321. Interesting photos; only covers Furness, Cockersand, Sawley, Whalley from Lancs. [LCL]

Clapham, Alfred W. Some famous buildings and their story : being the result of recent research in London and elsewhere, by Alfred W. Clapham and Walter H. Godfrey. Publisher Technical Journals, [19] Subject Cockersand Abbey. See "Cockersand Abbey and its chapter house" (pp. 105-116). [LCL]

McNulty, Joseph. Who was William Staynford - the abbot of the screen in Mitton

Church ? / by Joseph McNulty Historic Society of Lancashire & Cheshire Transactions 1939 vol.91 1939 p177-9 Location: Great Mitton; Cockersand Believed to be abbot of Cockersand Abbey [LL]

McNulty, Joseph. Who was William Staynford- abbot? / by Joseph McNulty Lancashire & Cheshire Antiquarian Society Transactions 1939 vol.54 1939 pp. 205-6 Stainford, William; McNulty, Joseph. Relates to Cockersand and Sawley abbeys [LL]

Cockersand Abbey. Lancaster Guardian 2 February 1934 Page Nos: 8 Illustrated. Photograph of Cockersand Abbey and details of its history. [LL]

The Times, Wednesday, Aug 18, 1926; pg. 13; Issue 44353; col B Cockersand Abbey. New Finds By Exploration Committee. [LCLDL and HLP]

Valuation lists: Cockersand Abbey RDLa 9/16 1911; Cockersand Abbey RDLa 9/17 1916-1919; Cockersand Abbey RDLa 9/18 1926. [LRO]

Ancient Monuments Society. Cockersand Abbey Exploration Committee. The third report and appeal for funds of the Cockersand Abbey Exploration Committee. Publisher [Ancient Monuments Society], [1926] [LCL]

Second report of the Cockersand Abbey Exploration Committee RCTm 5/10 1925 Jul. Photographs. Buck's engraving, 1727. Drawing Chapter House interior, etc. [LRO]

Swarbrick, John. The Abbey of St. Mary-of-the-Marsh at Cockersand. Manchester : Rawson, 1925. Reprinted from the "Transactions of the Lancashire and Cheshire Antiquarian Society, Vol. 40, 1922 & 1923. Describes wild nature of site, local sandstone etc. 2 ancient fishing baulks still there in 1923. [LCL]

The Times, Friday, Aug 14, 1925; pg. 7; col F Cockersand Abbey. Interesting Discoveries. [LCLDL and HLP]

First report of the Cockersand Abbey Exploration Committee of the Ancient Monuments Society RCTm 5/9 1924 Jun. Includes four photographs; plan of site. [LRO]

Recent excavations of the Abbey and grounds. Discovery of stone coffins. Preston Guardian 20 Sept 1924 p 3 Illus. Cols: a-f Cockersand Abbey [LL]

The Times, Friday, Sep 12, 1924; pg. 13; Issue 43755; col D Cockersand Abbey. Exploration of the ruins. [LCLDL and HLP]

The Times, Wednesday, Sep 03, 1924; pg. 15; col D. Cockersand Abbey. Results Of Recent Excavations. [LCLDL and HLP]

The Times, Monday, Aug 18, 1924; pg. 13; col B. Cockersand Abbey. Exploration Work. [LCLDL and HLP]

Excavations of the Abbey and grounds. Preston Guardian 1 September 1923 Page: 6 Illustrated. Cols : e-f Cockersand Abbey [LL]

Swarbrick, John. The Abbey of St. Mary of the Marsh at Cockersand / by John Swarbrick. Lancashire & Cheshire Antiquarian Society Transactions 1923 vol.40 1922-3 p163-93 [LL]

The Times, Tuesday, Jul 17, 1923; pg. 8; Issue 43395; col D. Cockersand Abbey. W. A. Wickham. [LCLDL and HLP]

The Times, Saturday, Jul 14, 1923; pg. 6; Issue 43393; col F . Cockersand Abbey. Photograph of stones believed to have come from the Abbey. [LCLDL and HLP]

Newdigate, C. A. Who was 'William Stainford - Abbot' ? / by C. A. Newdigate. Historic Society of Lancashire & Cheshire Transactions. 1917 vol.69 1917 p68-70 Location: Great Mitton; Cockersand Relates to a screen in Mitton Church reputed to have come from Cockersand Abbey [LL]

Wickham, W. A. Cockersand chapter house / by W. A. Wickham Historic Society of Lancashire & Cheshire Transactions 1915 vol.67 1915 p86-123 [LL]

Some notes on chapter-houses. W. A. Wickham. Volume: 64 (1912) Pages: 143-248, illus., plans, table. Includes much on Cockersand abbey chapter house, [http://www.hslc.org.uk/index_search.php?section=23&type=index]

19th Century

Cockersand Abbey RCHY 3/3 [no date] [LRO]

Roper, William Oliver. Cockersand Abbey. Photocopy from the "Transactions of the Lancashire and Cheshire Antiquarian Society" Vol. 4, 1886. [LCL]

Inventory of Whalley abbey. M. E. C. Walcott. Vol 19 (1866-1867) Pages: 103-110, Includes two items of plate remaining at Cockersand. [http://www.hslc.org.uk/index_search.php?section=23&type=index]

Lancaster. The Preston Chronicle (Preston, England), Saturday, April 11, 1857; Issue 2328 Stealing lead of 200lb weight from Cockersand Abbey. [LCLDL and HLP]

Excursion of the Liverpool Architectural and Archaeological Society to Whalley and Mitton Preston Chronicle Sat, July 1, 1854; Issue 2183. Screen of Little Mitton church brought from Cockersand Abbey. [LCLDL and HLP]

[Presentation and translation of a deed, on behalf of James Smith of Seaforth, concerning land in Scarisbrick. Walter of Scaresbreck to Cockersand abbey] by H. C. Pidgeon Volume: 2 (1849-1850) Pages: 214-215, http://www.hslc.org.uk/Search-Journals

John Weld's sketch book DP 386/1 1830-1836. A book of pencil, ink and watercolour sketches by John Weld of Leagram Hall during the period c.1830-1886. The subjects are ancient monuments, churches and country houses in Lancashire. Includes Cockersand. [LRO]

18th Century

Buck's views, including Cockersand abbey etc. 1727-1728. DP 189 [LRO]

15th Century and earlier

Leicester Abbey cartulary (Cockerham part). Subject Cockersand Abbey. [LCL]

Chetham Society. Remains... New series, Vol. 38 : The chartulary of Cockersand Abbey of the Premonstratensian Order, transcribed and edited by William Farrer. [Vol. 1], Part 1. Publisher C.S, 1898. ix - xxiv Introduction and history. All grants of land up to 1267. Latin, with English translations. [LCL]

Chetham Society. Remains... New series, Vol. 39 : The chartulary of Cockersand Abbey of the Premonstratensian Order, transcribed and edited by William Farrer. Vol. 1, Part 2. Publisher C.S, 1898. [LCL]

Chetham Society. Remains... New series, Vol. 40 : The chartulary of Cockersand Abbey of the Premonstratensian order, transcribed and edited by William Farrer. Vol. 2, Part 1. Publisher C.S, 1898. Also Vol 43. [LCL]

Chetham Society. Remains... New series, Vol. 56 : The chartulary of Cockersand Abbey of the Premonstratensian order, transcribed and edited by William Farrer. Publisher Manchester : C.S, 1905. [LCL]

Rentale de Cokersand : being the bursar's rent roll of the Abbey of Cokersand, in the County Palatine of Lancaster for the year 1501...edited by F.R. Raines. Publisher Chetham Soc, 1861. Reprinted from the Chetham Society's "Remains", 1st series, Vol. 57. Also Vol 64. [LCL]

Confirmation of grant 18 Jul 1310. By Edward II to Cockersand Abbey of a market to be held every Thursday, and a two day fair to be held on 28-29 Jun. each year at Garstang. CNP/6/1 [LRO]

Hesketh of Rufford c1200-1918. Various leases etc relating to Cockersand Abbey. DDHe [LRO]

Cockersand abbey deeds: Forton. c.1150-1504. DDX 161. Printed in Chetham Society, New Series, Vol. 40 [LRO]

Camden Society. Third series, vol. 6, Collectanea Anglo-Premonstratensia, vol. 1 : arranged and edited for the Royal Historical Society by Frances A. Gasquet. London : Royal Historical Society, 1904. xxxvi, 264 p. ; 22 cm. Premonstratensians - History - England - Sources. In Latin with preface and notes in English. Also Vol 2 Camden Society Vol 10, and Vol 3 - Camden Society Vol 12. Reports of Visitations of Premonstratensian houses. Volume 3 (Vol 12 in Camden Series) has an index to Vols 1 - 3; refs to Cockersand mainly in Vol 2. [LCL]

Appendix 15

Lancaster Priory

Please see Appendix 1 - General Sources for full details of the main sources of information, and full references. The General Sources are not included below

21st Century

Lancaster Priory Church website. Includes history, worship, services, etc. http://www.lancasterpriory.org/

20th Century

The PRIORY and parish church of the Blessed Mary of Lancaster, 1094-1994 : 900th anniversary service...20th November 1994....Includes historical notes. [LCL]

Colton. Holy Trinity Church. The registers of Colton 1813-1842, Lancaster Priory (marriages) 1754-1777 and Rusland 1782-1851 / [transcribed by Aidan C.J. Jones and others]. Series L.P.R.S.; 133 Publisher Lancs. Parish Register Soc, 1992. ISBN 1854451278 [LCL]

Look at Lancaster Priory. Publisher Doncaster : Bessacarr Prints, 1988. ISBN 0863841198 [LCL]

Tracy, Charles. Lancaster Priory choir stalls. Photocopy from Chapter 7 of "English Gothic choir stalls 1200-1400" by Charles Tracy: Boydell, 1987] [LCL]

McClintock, M. E. Lancaster Priory : the Church of the Blessed Mary of Lancaster. Publisher Pitkin Pictorial, 1980. Plan of church, with dates of sections. Many coloured photos, and detailed history. [LCL]

Cooper, L. I. The Priory Church of Saint Mary, Lancaster / [by L.I. Cooper and E.M.J. Cooper]. Publisher Lancaster : Saba Libris, 1972. [LCL]

Lancaster Assizes, 1176-1971 : the service before the opening of the last assizes to be held in the city on the occasion of the visit of Her Majesty's Judge of Assize, the Honourable Sir Joseph Donaldson Cantley, O.B.E., to Lancaster Priory and Parish Church on Tuesday, October 26th, 1971.... [LCL]

Photographs: "The Real Lancashire" 28 Mar 1965. DDEY/acc5582/36/5/9 Lancaster Priory Church. Duplicate in DDEY Box 36/6/42. [LRO]

Cowper, L. I. The priory and parish church of St. Mary, Lancaster, by L.I. & E.M.J. Cowper. Publisher Manchester : Holt Pub. Service, 1950. Guide. Includes table of chief events 78AD - 1946AD. [LCL]

Lectures on the antiquities and topography of Preston. The Preston Chronicle Sat, November 3, 1849; Issue 1940. In 958 the monks of the priory at Lancaster claimed the fishery of the Ribble in right of the Abbey of Lens in Normandy. [LCLDL]

Postcard of Lancaster Priory: St. Mary interior. DDX 391/14/51. No date. [LRO]

Lancaster Priory and Parish Church. Publisher [Manchester : Holt, 193 .] Blotter, including a history of the church and list of officers. [LCL]

The ceremony of laying up two stands of colours of the First Battalion the Royal Lancashire Militia, presented in 1806 and 1816, in the memorial chapel of the King's Own Royal Regiment in Lancaster Priory Church: Sunday Sept 18th, 1932. Publisher Lancaster : Castle Press (printer), 1932. Order of service. [LCL]

Bardsley, J. U. N. The priory and parish church of Lancaster: a handbook for pilgrims. 2nd ed. Publisher Lancaster : Wigley (printer), 1928. [LCL]

Wand, J. W. C. A short history of the priory and parish church of Lancaster. Publisher Lancaster : J.M. Wigley (printer), 1913. [LCL]

Lancaster jottings. HSCL, Vol 65 (1913) pp. 190-193, illus. Information on Lancaster priory. Mainly about 15C period after priory ceased. [LCL]

The priory and parish church of St Mary, Lancaster. Lancaster : Barber, [19] [LCL]

19th Century

Lancaster Priory and Parish Church. Lancaster : Wigley (Printer). [LCL]

John Weld's sketch book DP 386/1 1830-1836. A book of pencil, ink and watercolour sketches by John Weld of Leagram Hall during the period c.1830-1886. Includes Page: 15 description: Lancaster, Castle & Church [LRO]

Charters for Hornby Priory; Lancaster Priory. Subject: Baines Manuscript Collection. Handwritten transcription in Latin and English.- BAI C 72 12. [LCL]

Foundation of Lytham Priory, [1336] - [1444]. Subject Baines Manuscript Collection. Handwritten transcription.- .....Lancaster: Charter of Roger de Poietiers for good of his and relations' souls, gave, St Mary of Lancaster... [LCL]

Priory of Holland no. 1. Subject Baines Manuscript Collection. Upholland Priory. Handwritten copy in Latin and English. - .....Alien Priory of Lancaster. [LCL]

15th Century and earlier

Cartulary of the Benedictine priory of Blessed Mary of Lancaster with foundation, royal, episcopal, papal, and other charters. 2nd quarter of the 15th century [BL Catalogue of Illuminated Manuscripts - http://molcat1.bl.uk/illcat/record.asp?MSID=7367&CollID=8&NStart=3764 :

Detail Record for Harley 3764 (from BL Illuminated Manuscripts -) [http://www.bl.uk/catalogues/illuminatedmanuscripts/record.asp?MSID=7367&CollID=8&NStart=3764]

Grant from the Abbot of Combermere and others to Lancaster Priory of land at Crosby E3.11/1/2 [13th century]. [Chetham Library]

Copy of Lancaster Priory chartulary. PR3262/14/85, PR3262/14/86. Transcription and translation in: Materials for the History of the Church of Lancaster, volume. 1, ed. W.O. Roper, Chetham Society, 1892, volume. 26, pp. 7-20. Includes the original Latin and a translation. British Museum manuscript has 82 pages. Also Vol 31. [LRO]

Appendix 16

Lancaster Friars

Please see Appendix 1 - General Sources for full details of the main sources of information, and full references. The General Sources are not included below

20th Century
PARKIN, Wilfred. The Friars Preachers in Lancashire, 1260-1990. Excalibur, 1991. ISBN 185634097X. [LCL]

Penney, S. H.; Greene, J.; Noake, Beryl. 'Excavations at Lancaster Friary'. Contrebis: a bulletin of archaeology for Lancashire and the North-West, 10 (1982), 1-13. Lancaster Archaeological Society. ISSN 0307-5087. [LCL]

19th Century
Notes on the ancient religious houses of the County of Lancaster. Dom. G. Dolan HSLC Volume: 43 (1891-1892) pp 201-232 [www.hslc.org.uk/]

Palmer, C. F. R. The friar-preachers, or, Blackfriars, of Lancaster. Publisher Bemrose (printers), 1885. Subject: Dominicans. Excerpt from "The reliquary, quarterly archaeology journal and review" No.101, vol.26 July 1885.- Some pages missing. [LCL]

Grant of charters to Prior of Cockerham, Warrington; foundation of the Collegiate Church at Manchester; Lancaster (Black Friars); Preston (Grey Friars). Subject: Baines Manuscript Collection. Handwritten copy of extract from Dugdale's Monasticon. - BAI C 71 21 [LCL]

16th Century
Ministers Accounts, Exchequer, relating to the property of the Grey Friars, Preston, and the Augustine Friars, Lancaster P/13 1539. PRO copy held in Lancashire Record Office; gloves recommended! In Latin. [LRO]

15th Century and earlier
Affidavit of certain persons made in the Church of the Friars of Lancaster. D PEN/BUNDLE 47/27 1491 7th Henry VII 17th November [CAS and Local Studies Library, Whitehaven]

Appendix 17

Lancaster Hospitals

Please see Appendix 1 - General Sources for full details of the main sources of information, and full references. The General Sources are not included below

20th Century

Glover, Barbara M. Lancaster charities. Author, 1952. Friends Meeting House - Penny's Charity- Almshouses - Heysham's Charity - Gardyner's Charity - Schools - Hospitals. Duplicated typescript in folder.- Includes plans of sites of charities' property, drawing of the Friend's Meeting House. [LCL]

Great Britain. Charity Commission. In the matter of the following charities, in the borough of Lancaster, in the county of Lancaster: 1. The almshouse and pension charities...2. The Ecclesiastical Charity for the Reader...3. The charity of Charles Blades for Poor Men...and, In the matter of "The Charitable Trusts Acts, 1853 to 1894".... London : Eyre & Spottiswoode for H.M.S.O., [1913]. + several other reports. [LCL]

Image of Gardyner's Almshouses, St Mary's Gate, c 1900. [LL]

19th Century

Leprosy and Local Leper Hospitals, by Henry Barnes. Vol 10, Old Series, CWAAS, 1889, p 100. Brief mention only of Lancaster. More details of other hospitals at Carlisle, Appleby and Kendal. [LRO]

Applicants for Gardyner's Charity, 6th April, 1864 - July 21st, 1868. Printed lists of names, ages, addresses and trades. [LCL]

Lancaster Charities. [Copy of the Master's report, July 24, 1837, and the Lord Chancellor's order, August 10th, 1837]. Report on the Penny, Heysham, Gardyner, Gillison, France and Harrison charities and almshouses, and Pyper's charity and National School. Also Report for 25 Aug, 1837. [LCL]

Foundation of Lytham Priory, [1336] - [1444]. Baines Manuscript Coll. Handwritten transcription.- BAI C 72 11. Includes Lancaster Hospital. [LCL]

House of Commons Papers, 1833: Lancaster, Charitable Funds: [http://books.google.co.uk/books] (Search for Gardyner's + Lancaster)

Appendix 18

Cartmel Priory

Please see Appendix 1 - General Sources for full details of the main sources of information, and full references. The General Sources are not included below

21st Century

Cartmel Priory website. Includes current information, and history etc. [http://www.cartmelpriory.org.uk/Home]

Cartmel Priory Gatehouse. http://www.visitcumbria.com/sl/cartmel-priory-gatehouse/

Transactions of the Cumberland and Westmorland Antiquarian and Archaeological Society: Index 1866 - 2005. Many articles. [http://cumbriapast.com/cgi-bin/ms/main.pl?action=transactions]

Wild, Chris and Howard-Davis, Christine. Excavations at Priory Gardens Cartmel Cumb & Westmorland Antiquarian & Archaeological Society Trans 2000 vol. 100 pp 161-180 Illustrated. Excavations to NW of church, within precinct of priory; found significant medieval, probably monastic, activity. [LCL]

Lancashire Churches, by Tony Boughen. Includes Cartmel Priory Church [http://www.lancashirechurches.co.uk/index.htm]

Hebgin-Barnes, Penny. The medieval stained glass of Lancashire. Oxford: Oxford University Press, 2009. ISBN: 0197264484, 9780197264485.

Cartmel Priory: ancient jewel, living church. Ruddocks Publishing, 2015. ISBN: 9780904327106.

Smith, R. The Priory Church of St Mary and St Michael, Cartmel Priory, Cumbria. Wenlock, Shropshire, RJL Smith & Associates, 2007. ISBN: 187155489.

20th Century

Cartmel Priory CC/EVS/1/4. No date. [LRO].

Dickinson, J. C. The priory of Cartmel. Publisher Cicerone, 1991. ISBN 1852840773 [LCL]

Cartmel Priory: watching brief in 1991 for Cartmel Parochial Church Council, report November 1992. WDSo 185/6 1991 [CASK]

Baker, T. Cartmel Priory: the Priory Church of St Mary and St Michael, Cartmel. Cartmel Parochial Church Council, 1991. [CCL]

Wilson, P R and Clare, T Farmery Field Cartmel Cumberland & Westmorland Antiquarian & Archaeological Society Transactions 1990 vol. 90 pp 195-198 Illustrated. [LL]

Dickinson, J. C. A fourteenth-century painted wooden tester from Cartmel Priory and seventeenth-century sculpture from Furness Abbey, Cumbria / [by] J.C. Dickinson and Paul Willliamson. Reprinted from "The Antiquaries Journal", Vol. 65, Part 2, 1985: "Exhibits at Ballots", p. 473-474. [LCL]

Dickinson, J. C. The land of Cartmel: a history. Titus Wison, 1980. 0900811129. [CCL]

Dickinson, J. C. A new guide to Cartmel Priory Church. Edition 2nd ed. Publisher Sandside : Holdsworth (Printer). [LCL]

Dickinson, J. C. A new guide to Cartmel priory church. The Author, 1945. [CCL]

Dickinson, J. C. The story of the priory church of St. Mary the Virgin, Cartmel. Publisher Gloucester : British Pub. Co. [LCL]

Dickinson, J. C. The story of the Priory Church of St Mary, Cartmel. Cartmel Priory, 1933. [CCL]

Dykes, L. G. F. The Priory Church of St. Mary, Cartmel : a short descriptive and historical note, by L.G.F. Dykes and T. Hardwick. Edition [New ed.] Grange-Over-Sands : J. Wadsworth (Printer), [19] [LCL]

Dykes, L.G.F. The Priory Church of St. Mary and St. Michael, Cartmel : a short descriptive and historical note by L.G.F. Dykes and T. Hardwick. 13th ed. Grange-Over-Sands : J. Wadsworth (Printer), [19] + earlier editions. [LCL]

Guide book to Cartmel Priory, c 1960. BDX 296/8/6 [CASB]

Cartmel Priory Church. Photographs. Black and white. No date. DRC/56/1/2/55-59. [CASB]

Cartmel Priory. Glass negatives. No's 61-62. No date. WDB 86/11/1. [CASK]

Cartmel Priory. Printed history with illustrations. c. 1960. BDX 471/1/3. [CASB]

Taylor, Sam. The ancient library in Cartmel Priory Church. University Library, 1959. [CCL]

Letters about Cartmel Priory Library WPR 89/1/4/17 1910-1956 [CASK]

Taylor, Sam. Cartmel, people and Priory. Titus Wilson, 1955. [CCL]

Chaplin, W. R. M. The bells of the priory church of St. Mary and St. Michael, Cartmel. Publisher Kendal : Wilson, [19] [LCL]

Guide to Grange and the neighbourhood with notes on Cartmel Priory Church, Lancashire. Publisher Cartmel : Brockbank (Printer), [19] Notes on Cartmel Priory Church by F.A. Paley. [LCL]

Wells, R. Notes on the priory church of S. Mary, Cartmel. [LCL]

Monumental inscriptions in old churchyard of Cartmel Priory and inside church, by David Ensign Gardner, Liverpool, October 1939. WDY 224/2. [CASK]

The Times, Saturday, Sep 05, 1936; pg. 6; Issue 47472; col B. Visitors To Churches Charges For Admission C. K. Burton. [LCLDL]

Wallis, John Eyre Winstanley. The narrative of the indictment of the traitors of Whalley and Cartmell, 1536-7. Publisher Manchester : Chetham Soc, 1931. Subject Whalley Abbey - Cartmel Priory. Reprinted from "Remains Historical and Literary..." of Chetham Societ, new series, vol. 90, 1931. [LCL]

The Times, Thursday, Jan 29, 1931; pg. 8; Issue 45733; col G. Alleged Theft Of Rare Book [LCLDL]

Pearson, R. O'Neill. Cartmel Priory Gate House. Publisher Ulverston : Fletcher & Robinson (Printers), 1923. [LCL]

The Times, Friday, Jun 29, 1923; pg. 14; Issue 43380; col E. An Ancient Priory. Cartmel Gatehouse to be opened. [LCLDL]

Cartmel Priory Church, Cartmel. Measured drawing showing east elevation AL0250/171/03 1911 - 1920 [EHNMR]

Wakefield, A. M. Cartmel Priory and sketches of North Lonsdale. H.T. Mason, 1909. [CCL]

19th Century

Cooper- Rev. Canon George Preston and Cartmel Priory Church / by Rev. Canon Cooper Historic Society of Lancashire & Cheshire Transactions 1899 vol.51 1899 p221-7 [LL]

Notes & Queries. Manchester Times (Manchester, England), Friday, April 8, 1898; Issue 2121. Tradition, of beginnings of priory. [LCLDL]

Guide Book: Illustrated handbook to Cark-in-Cartmel, Flookburgh, Holker Hall, Cartmel Priory Church. 1895. BDX 342/9/1. [CASB]

Cartmel. Manchester Times (Manchester, England), Saturday, September 7, 1889; Issue 1676. Quite a lot about the priory, etc. [LCLDL]

Cartmel Priory Church. Ulverston, 1887. [CCL]

Country Life Manchester Times (Manchester, England), Saturday, February 13, 1886; Issue 1492 Cartmel Fell Church. [LCLDL]

Rigge, H. F. Cartmel Priory Church, North Lancashire. E. Wilson, 1885. Also earlier ed 1879. [CCL]

Cartmel Priory Church. The Leeds Mercury (Leeds, England), Saturday, May 10, 1884; Issue 14380. History, including pre-Conquest and St Cuthbert. [LCLDL]

Holt, J. G. Cartmel Priory: buildings before the Dissolution. Edward Gill, 1881. [CCL]

Rigge, Henry Fletcher. A paper on the Harrington tomb in Cartmel Priory Church, read before the members of the Cumb and Westmorland Antiquarian and Archaeological Society. Publisher: Kendal : Wilson (Printer), 1881. [LCL]

Photocopy of "The Older Monuments in Cartmel Priory Church" by Henry

Fletcher Rigge. 1876. WDY 224/1. [CASK]

Hubbersty, R. C. A statement of subscriptions and expenditure on account of the restoration and improvement of the Priory Church of St Mary, Cartmel since the year 1864.... Cartmel : Brickel (Printer), 1873. [LCL]

Paley, F.A. Architectural notes on Cartmel Priory church. W Brickel, 1872. [CCL]

Stockdale, James. Annales Caermoelenses; or annals of Cartmel. William Kitchin, Ulverston, 1872. Includes a short history of the priory up to the Dissolution. [CCL].

James Stockdale's historical research papers for Annals of Cartmel. 1685-1873. DDHJ 4/2/1. [CASB]

Over Sands to the Lakes. Manchester Times Sat, June 2, 1860; Issue N/A. Supposed origins of Cartmel Priory, St Bernard's Mount etc. [LCLDL]

Cartmel Priory Church, Lancashire. Cartmel : H Brockbank, 1857. [LCL]

John Weld's sketch book DP 386/1 1830-1836 A book of pencil, ink and watercolour sketches by John Weld of Leagram Hall during the period c.1830-1886. The subjects are ancient monuments, churches and country houses in Lancashire. Includes Page: 25 & Page 26: Cartmel Priory choir & Harrington monument [LRO]

18th Century

Cartmel Church organ. Photocopy of note about ....Cartmel Church organ by William Field, August 1796. WDY 580. [CASK]

Buck's views of Cartmel priory, etc. DP 189 1727-1728 [LRO]

Engravings: Cumberland, Lancashire and Westmorland 1727-1904. Includes Cartmel priory (1727). Z/3393. [CASB]

17th Century

[no title] WPR 89/1/4/16 1833 Contents: A Translation from the Latin of Letters Patent of Charles I... granting lands of dissolved Priory of Cartmel to seven principal landholders, 1 July 16 Charles I [1641]. [CASK]

Cartmel. Grant in fee farm of lands of Cartmel Priory manuscript. 1640. Z/1495. [CASB]

Appendix 19

Conishead Priory

Please see Appendix 1 - General Sources for full details of the main sources of information, and full references. The General Sources are not included below

21st Century

Conishead Priory website. [http://www.conisheadpriory.org/]

Manjushri Kadampa Meditation Centre website. International Buddhist Meditation Centre and Temple for World Peace. [http://nkt-kmc-manjushri.org/]

Transactions of the Cumberland and Westmorland Antiquarian and Archaeological Society: Index 1866 - 2005. Many articles. [http://cumbriapast.com/cgi-bin/ms/main.pl?action=transactions]

Holmes, Sarah Elizabeth. The Paradise of Furness: the story of Conishead Priory and its people. Handstand Press, 2012. ISBN: 0955200989, 9780955200984. [LCL]Upholland priory

20th Century

The Story of Conishead Priory, Ulverston. Rev. ed. Ulverston : Atkinson, 1950. Mansion built on the site of a medieval priory, converted into a convalescent home in the 1950s. [LCL]

The story of Conishead Priory, Ulverston. James Atkinson, Ulverston, 1931. + revised edition, 1950. [CCL]

"Excavations at Conishead Priory" by P V Kelly. In: CWAAS vol XXX, 1930, pp 149-168. BDX 53/2/4. Includes plan showing the church excavations, south of the present mansion. [CASB]

The Times, Saturday, Feb 02, 1929; pg. 15; Issue 45117; col F Conishead Priory. Church Ruins Discovered. [LCLDL]

Lord Harington and Conishead William Harington Historic Society of Lancashire and Cheshire Transactions 1922 Vol 74 pp. 152 [LL]

19th Century

Conishead Priory, photograph. General exterior view from afar (General view) OP02325 01 Jan 1860 - 31 Dec 1900 [EHNMR]

Philp, Dr. Guide to Conishead Priory and the surrounding district. Publisher Edinburgh : Bartholomew, 1880. Conishead Priory, a mansion built 1821, is on the site of a medieval religious foundation. [LCL]

New Hydropathic Establishment The Preston Chronicle etc (Preston, England), Saturday, April 12, 1879; Issue 3451 [LCLDL]

Conishead Priory Liverpool Mercury etc (Liverpool, England), Monday, April 7, 1879; Issue 9744. [LCLDL]

Local News The Preston Chronicle etc (Preston, England), Saturday, April 5, 1879; Issue 3450 Opening Dinner of Conishead Priory Hydropathic Establishment. [LCLDL]

Latest ... News Liverpool Mercury etc (Liverpool, England), Saturday, November 30, 1878; Issue 9635 Bones found, not monks. [LCLDL]

Holker Hall, seat of the Duke of Devonshire, destroyed by fire yesterday The Preston Chronicle etc Saturday, March 11, 1871; Issue 3114. [LCLDL]

Agreement for lease of Conishead Priory BPR 2/M/10 1867 [CASB]

Over Sands to the Lakes Manchester Times (Manchester, England), Saturday, June 2, 1860; Issue N/A. [LCLDL]

Multum in Parvo Liverpool Mercury etc (Liverpool, England), Tuesday, October 12, 1852; Issue 2440 Sold to Askew. [LCLDL]

Local Intelligence The Preston Chronicle etc (Preston, England), Sat, Sept 21, 1850; Issue 1989. Lots for sale from priory. + Oct 5th. [LCLDL]

Engravings and maps: Lancashire and Westmorland 1785-1850 Collection of engravings and maps including a book of engravings (Includes Conishead Priory). Z/3403 [CASB]

Conishead Priory estate. 1777-1852. Z/3180. [CASB]

Transcript from the title deeds etc of Conishead Priory Estate. Also suit of Petty and Postlethwaite vs Braddyl, compiled by James Park. 1777-1852. BDX 53/7. [CASB]

Multum in Parvo Liverpool Mercury etc (Liverpool, England), Tuesday, January 1, 1850; Issue 2155. Greyhound dropped dead! [LCLDL]

Conishead Priory and upwards of 42½ acres of land, near Ulverston, in (Property) The Times Saturday, Oct 07, 1848; p. 12; Iss 19988; col A [LCLDL]

Bundles: individual deeds; exemplification of recovery 12 February 1768; copy mortgages etc.; insurance policy on Conishead Priory 1847; Conishead estates; Gale and Braddyll families. 1668-1847. BDX 209/1/34. [CASB]

The tourist's manual packet guide to the lakes of Lancashire, Westmorland and Cumberland. John Jackson, 1845. [CCL]

Three Days in Furness The Preston Chronicle etc (Preston, England), Saturday, August 31, 1844; Issue 1670. [LCLDL]

Survey of religious houses - First and second values; Bells, lead and woods; Woods worth to be sold; No. of religious persons, their debts, servants and others, and their offer of redemption.Includes Conishead, etc. [Harleian Codex 604.]. Subject Baines Manuscript Collection. BAI A 21 [LCL]

"Historical and Descriptive Account of Conishead Priory", from the Lonsdale Magazine and Kendal Repository. 1822. BDX 53/2/2. [CASB]

Bond in Â£4000 to be paid to John Machell of Pennybridge by Wilson Braddyll of Conishead Priory, esq., and Thomas Braddyll of Hampton Court, esq., 16 February 1814. BDHJ/2/2/18. [CASB]

Wilson Braddyll of Conishead Priory QSQ/3/7/2 18 Dec 1803 [LRO]

Diaries of William Fleming of Pennington 1800-1821 Diaries and commonplace books of William Fleming of Pennington 1800-1821 (9 volumes); includes printed sale catalogue of furniture and books at Conishead Priory (1 volume). BDX 584. [CASB]

18th Century

News World (1787) (London, England), Thursday, September 10, 1789; Issue 838 Brief mention of Braddyl and Duke of York. [LCLDL]

Copy of will of Thomas Bradyll of Stratton Street, Piccadilly, Middlesex, and also of Conishead Priory. Will dated 1 April 1776; "Obt. July 1776." BDX 209/3/13. [CASB]

1. Francis Morice of City of Westminster, Middx esq., and Francis Phelipe of London, gent. 2. John Corney of Orton, clerk, Edmund Branthwaite of Carlingill, gent and Philip Winster of Borrowbridge, yeoman, [both Orton]. Premises: all the rectory of Orton with members and appurtenances with all tithes of yearly value of Â£20 parcel of the possessions of the late Priory of Conishead; and the advowson and patronage of the church of Orton. - With 18th. cent. copy of deed. [113a]. WPR 9/2/2/1. [CAS]

Translation of Final Concord 1. Alexander Osbaldeston Esquire, William Kirkby Esquire, Richard Gough Esquire, Joseph Hodges Bart., plaintiffs. 2. Joseph Braddyll Esquire, and Sarah his wife, deforciants. The Manor of Salmesbury and the seite of the dissolved Priory of Conishead, 82 messuages, 80 cottages, 2 water corn mills and other premises in Lancashire 18 August 1 Geo. 1714. BDX 209/1/40. [CASB]

17th Century

Bundle of "old probates and deeds relating to Conishead Priory." 17th century - 18th century. BDX 209/1/25. [CASB]

Counterpart deed of entail: former priory of Conishead, 1602 1. Gyles Brownerigge of the parish of St Clement Danes, Middlesex, tayllor and Humfrey Hooper of the parish of St Dunstan, Cittie of London, stacyoner. 2. Myles Doddinge the elder of Conishead, Lancashire, esquire and Margaret his wife, Myles Doddinge the younger, gent, Robert Doddinge, gent, and another son of Myles. Premises: moiety of former priory of Conishead. BDX 209/2/31/3 [CASB]

Bundle of deeds. 1603-1711 Leases of Conishead Priory, 1 November 1650 and 24 March 1711; conveyance of a moiety of Conishead, 19 March 1603/4; conveyance of a lease of 60 years of a moiety of Conishead, 27 November 1631; covenant to levy a fine on the manor of Conishead and premises at Dalton...I August 1633. BDX 209/1/22. [CASB]

16th Century
........Premises:- all tithes of corn, grain and sheaves due to the Rector and also all tithes of calves, chickens and milk called White tithes or White soule tithes and all tithes of oblations and other profits, lately belonging to the Priory of the Blessed Virgin Mary of Conishead in co. Lancs....Auditor of the Duchy of Lancaster, 24 November 1586. WPR 9/3/1/1. [CAS]
> Rigge family papers, 1581-1880. DDHJ/3. [CASB]
> Rawlinson family papers, 1551-c1890. DDHJ/2. [CASB]

15th Century and earlier
Transcripts of Conishead Priory documents from 1318 Patent Roll. Z/100/1. [CASB]

Appendix 20

Furness Abbey

Please see Appendix 1 - General Sources for full details of the main sources of information, and full references. The General Sources are not included below

21st Century
Barrow in Furness Civic and Local History Society. Useful introduction. especially for schools. [http://www.furnessabbey.org.uk/home%20page.html]
Photographs. [http://www.visitcumbria.com/sl/furness-abbey/]
Visitor information:
[http://www.english-heritage.org.uk/daysout/properties/furness-abbey/]
Cistercians in Yorkshire Project, but information on other Cistercian houses too, including Furness, Sawley and Whalley,
[http://cistercians.shef.ac.uk/abbeys/furness.php]
Morrison, John. Morecambe Bay. Londlon: Frances Lincoln, 2008. Illustrated. Includes Furness Abbey and Cartmel Priory. [CCL]
Transactions of the Cumberland and Westmorland Antiquarian and Archaeological Society: Index 1866 - 2005. Many articles.
[http://cumbriapast.com/cgi-bin/ms/main.pl]
Freeman, Elizabeth. Models for Cistercian Life in Jocelin of Furness's Vita Waldevi. Cistercian Studies Quarterly, 37:2, 2002, p 107-121. [EBSCOHost]
Dade-Robertson, Christine. Furness Abbey : romance, scholarship and culture. Publisher Lancaster : Centre for North-West Regional Studies, 2000. ISBN 1862200955. [LCL]

20th Century
Harrison, Stuart. Furness Abbey. English Heritage, 1998. ISBN 1850746745. [CCL]
Hoyle, R.W. & Summerson, H.R.T. The Earl of Derby and the Deposition of the

Abbot of Furness in 1514. Northern History Vol 30, Jan 1994, p 184-192. [EBSCOHost]

Dickinson, J. C. Furness Abbey, Cumbria. 4th ed. ISBN 1850741301. English Heritage, 1989. [CCL]

Leach, Alice. Furness Abbey: a history and illustrated guide. Furness Heritage Press, 1988. [CCL]

Furness Abbey. Furness Museum, 1987. Leaflet containing a short history of the abbey and details of opening times and admission prices. [LCL]

Dickinson, J. C. A fourteenth-century painted wooden tester from Cartmel Priory and seventeenth-century sculpture from Furness Abbey, Cumbria / [by] J.C. Dickinson and Paul Williamson. Reprinted from "The Antiquaries Journal", Vol. 65, Part 2, 1985: "Exhibits at Ballots", p. 473-474. [LCL]

Dickinson, J. C. Furness Abbey, Lancashire. HMSO, 1982. ISBN 0116701374. [CCL]

The Times, Monday, Sep 25, 1978; pg. 15; Issue 60415; col A. Seekers Of Solitude In Crowds. Wordsworth and Furness Abbey. [LCLDL]

Dickinson, J. C. Furness Abbey, Lancashire. London : H.M.S.O., 1965. ISBN 0116701374 Includes folded plan of the abbey. [LCL]

The Times, Saturday, Aug 27, 1955; pg. 8; Issue 53310; col E. Over The Sands: Exploring An Old Coach-Way Round Morecambe Bay. [LCLDL]

Knowles, David. Monastic sites from the air, by David Knowles and J.K.S. St Joseph. C.U.P, 1952. Search Room. H321. Interesting photos; only covers Furness, Cockersand, Sawley, Whalley from Lancashire. [LCL]

Garton, S. J. Ancient Monuments and Historic Buildings - Furness Abbey. HMSO, 1950. [CCL]

Garton, S. J. Furness Abbey. Publisher London : HMSO, 1947. Short guide with itinerary and plan for visiting the remains of the abbey. [LCL]

McKean, John. A report on the historical value of the Coucher Book of Furness Abbey. The author, 1935. Thesis (M.A.). - Duplicated typescript. Spine title: Historical value of the Furness Abbey Coucher Book. [LCL]

The Times, Friday, Jul 19, 1935; pg. 15; Issue 47120; col G . Relics In Stone A Record Of Good Guardianship, Three Ancient English Abbeys. From a Correspondent. Includes Furness. [LCLDL]

The Times, Monday, Sep 15, 1930; pg. 9; col F Furness Cowcher Book Lost Page Restored After Centuries. In PRO [LCLDL]

Hope, John. The Abbey of St Mary in Furness, Lancashire. Cumberland and Westmorland Ant Vol XVI, 1929. [CCL]

The granges of Furness Abbey. Historic Society of Lancashire and Cheshire Transactions 1928 Volume (Issue): 80 pp 58-85. Source mainly Coucher Book of Furness Abbey. Has map showing location of all granges. [LL]

The Times, Monday, Jul 18, 1927; pg. 11; Issue 44636; col B. Furness Abbey. 800th Anniversary Of The Founding. [LCLDL]

The Times, Saturday, Jul 16, 1927; pg. 13; Issue 44635; col G Furness Abbey. King Stephen's Charter. After 800 Years. [LCLDL]

The Times, Saturday, Jul 16, 1927; pg. 21; Issue 44635; col A The Programmes. Furness Abbey. [LCLDL]

Grange-Over-Sands. The Rose-Red Abbey Of Furness. (News) The Times Friday, Aug 07, 1925; pg. 15; Issue 44034; col E. [LCLDL]

The Times, Friday, Mar 11, 1921; pg. 10; Issue 42666; col F. Ruins at a Gift....Work

Of Preservation Furness offered to State. [LCLDL]

A plan by Barrow Council to restore Furness Abbey. Preston Guardian 11-Sep-1920 Page: 6. [LL]

Johnson, Thomas. A gossiping guide to Morecambe, Heysham, Silverdale, Arnside, Grange, Cartmel, Ulverston, Furness Abbey, Lancaster, Kirby Lonsdale and the valley of the Lune. Blackburn : Author (Printer), [ ] [LCL]

Beauty and Destruction. (Editorials/Leaders) The Times Monday, May 31, 1915; pg. 7; Issue 40868; col B [LCLDL]

Suppression of the Monastery of Furness, 1537, by W B Kendall. 1909. ZK/207. [CASB]

The English Lake District including Furness Abbey, Shap Spa, Seascale etc etc. Series The concise series of guides; No. 1. Publisher Edinburgh: Menzies. 1908? [LCL]

Concise guide to the English Lakes with maps and views: including Furness Abbey.... Titus Wilson, Kendal, 1908. [CCL]

Pearson, R. O'Neill. Furness Abbey : paper read...before the Cumberland and Westmorland Antiquarian and Archaeological Society, at Carlisle, on 18th April, 1907 on "The dispute between the abbots of Furness and Savigny in the light of 12th century documents now at Paris". Publisher Ulverston : Atkinson (Printer), 1907. [LCL]

A guide to Coniston, the Old Man, and the lakes and fells; with a description of Furness Abbey and Barrow-in-Furness. Series Abel Heywood's series of illustrated penny guide books. Manchester : London : Abel Heywood ; E.W. Allen, 1903. Cover title: Coniston and Furness Abbey illustrated. [LCL]

Hope, William Henry St. John. The Abbey of St. Mary in Furness, Lancashire. Publisher Kendal : Titus Wilson, 1902. [LCL]

On the first church at Furness. Lancashire and Cheshire Antiquarian Society Transactions. 1900 Volume (Issue): 18 pp 70-87 [LL]

19th Century

Sydney, William Connor. Furness Abbey and its Story. Gentleman's Magazine 280:1981, Jan 1896, p. 89-98. [British Periodicals Collection, UMI]

Barber, Henry. The tourist's guide to Furness Abbey and its vicinity. Edition 5th ed. Publisher Ulverston : Atkinson, [ ] [LCL]

Morris, J. P. A handy guide to the ruins of Furness Abbey. Edition [Rev. ed.] / revised by J. Turner. Publisher Ulverston : J. Atkinson. [LCL]

Paley, F. A. A manual of Gothic moldings with directions for copying them and for determining their dates. Edition 5th ed. / with numerous additions by W.M. Fawcett. Publisher Gurney & Jackson, 1891. [LCL]

Waddington, T. A. J. Waddington's practical guide to Furness Abbey, Barrow, Ulverston, Cartmel... Waddington, 1890. [CCL]

Morris, J. P. A handy guide to the ruins of Furness Abbey. Publisher Ulverston : J. Atkinson, [1888] [LCL]

Ward and Lock's pictorial and historical guide to Morecambe Bay, Furness Abbey.... Ward, 1887. [CCL]

Furness Abbey The Leeds Mercury (Leeds, England), Saturday, July 26, 1884; Issue 14446. [LCLDL]

Ferguson, Richard S. Masons' marks from Furness and Calder Abbeys. Publisher Kendal : Wilson, 1883. [LCL]

The Times, Friday, Aug 26, 1881; pg. 10; Issue 30283; col C Furness Abbey. M. D.

K.. Category: Letters to the Editor [LCLDL]

Barber, Henry. Shaw's tourists' picturesque guide to Furness Abbey, the vicinity, and, Lakes Coniston and Windermere. Edition 8th ed. Publisher Norton & Shaw, [1876]. Some earlier eds. published as "The tourist's guide to Furness Abbey and its vicinity". [LCL]

Places of popular resort - Furness Abbey. London Journal 62:1598, 25 Sept 1875. p197-8. [British Periodicals Collection, UMI]

Furness Abbey. The Graphic (London, England), Saturday, September 12, 1874. Drawing of the sedilia. [LCLDL]

West Doorway, Furness Abbey The Graphic (London, England), September 12, 1874; Issue 250 Drawing. [LCLDL]

Mannex and Co. Directory of North and East Lancashire, &c. with historical sketches of Furness and Whalley Abbeys and the religious orders; .....&c Preston : P. Mannex, 1868. [LCL]

Paley, F.A. A manual of Gothic moldings with directions for copying them and for determining their dates. Edition 3rd ed. / with numerous additions by W.M. Fawcett. Publisher Van Voorst, 1865. Subject Furness Abbey. Lancaster author. - Includes examples from Furness Abbey. [LCL]

Payn, James. Furness Abbey and its neighbourhood : with photographs of the ruins. Publisher Simpkin, Marshall. [LCL]

Payn, James. A description of Furness Abbey and its neighbourhood. Hamilton, Adams & Co., 1864. [CCL]

Fletcher, Joseph. Collection of masons' marks from Furness Abbey, Lancashire. 1858. [CCL]

Carlyle, R. Six views of the ruins of Furness Abbey, Lancashire, with a compendious account of the monastery. Ulverston: Atkinson, 1858. [LCL]

A Lay of Furness Abbey. Chamber's Edinburgh Journal, 473 Jan 22 1853, p. 64. [British Periodicals Collection, UMI]

Furness Abbey. The Preston Chronicle, Saturday, August 31, 1850; Issue 1986. [LCLDL and HLP]

Furness Abbey. Sharpe's London Journal 12 July 1850, pp 1-2. [British Periodicals Collection, UMI]

A pleasure trip to Furness Abbey : by the steamer "Duchess of Lancaster", July 13th, 1848. Publisher Lancaster : Wigley (printer), 1895. [LCL]

Soulby, Stephen. Furness Abbey and the best way to see the lakes. Stephen Soulby, Ulverston, 1848. [CCL]

Furness Abbey guides, 1847-c.1860. Contents: A guide from Blackpool and Fleetwood to Furness Abbey (Fleetwood : W. Porter, 1847) -- A guide through the ruins of Furness Abbey (Ulverston : David Atkinson, 1854) -- A hand book to Furness Abbey (Ulverston : J. Jackson, [1860?]). 3 pamphlets bound in 1 vol. - 'A hand book to Furness Abbey' contains details of excavations of 1859 and a list of local plants and their habitats. [LCL]

Hand book to the Abbey of St Mary of Furness, in Lancashire. Stephen Soulby, 1845. [CCL]

Woodford, John. Tithes relating to tenements and lands in Borrodale, formerly under the Abbey of Furness.... T. Bailey, 1845. [CCL]

Beck, Alcock. Annales Furnesienses : history and antiquities of the abbey of Furness. Publisher Payne & Foss. 1844. [CCL]

Three days in Furness Preston Chronicle, Saturday, August 31, 1844; Issue 1670. [Lancashire County Library Online Reference Library and HLP]

Wright, Thomas. Three Chapters of Letters relating to the Suppression of Monasteries. Camden Society, 1843. Contains report of surrender of Furness Abbey. [CCL]

Furness Abbey. North of England Magazine and Bradshaw's Journal.... 20, Sept 1843, p. 275-276. Poem. [British Periodicals Collection, UMI]

Evans, Francis. Furness and Furness Abbey: a companion .... D. Atkinson, 1842. [CCL]

An Excursion to Fleetwood, Furness Abbey, &c., &c Preston Chronicle Saturday, July 16, 1842; Issue 1559. [LCLDL and HLP]

Ruins of Furness Abbey. Preston Chronicle, Saturday, June 18, 1842; Issue 1555. [LCLDL and HLP]

Furness Abbey, Lancashire. Saturday Magazine 20:630, 30 Apr 1842, P 161-163. [British Periodicals Collection, UMI]

A Hand-Book for Lake visitors with a new map of the Lake District; to which is appended an account of Furness Abbey and a ground plan of that building. Publisher Kendal : Hudson & Nicholson. 1841? + later editions in Cumbria County Library. [LCL]

View of Furness Abbey from the School-House - Interior of the Chapter-House, Furness Abbey. Literary Gazette 945, 28 Feb 1835, p. 138. [British Periodicals Collection, UMI]

Furness Abbey, Lancashire. Mirror of Literature, Amusement and Instruction, 21:594, Mar 9 1833, p. 145-146. [British Periodicals Collection, UMI]

A Hand Book to Furness Abbey : with a short account of the Pile of Fouldrey and Rampside : to which is appended a condensed description of the Lake District. Publisher Ulverston : J. Jackson, [18] [LCL]

John Weld's sketch book DP 386/1 1830-1836 A book of pencil, ink and watercolour sketches by John Weld of Leagram Hall during the period c.1830-1886. Includes Page: 12 Furness Abbey location; Page: 29 description: Furness Abbey, gravestones location; Page: 49 description; effigies. [LRO]

Furness Abbey, in the Vale of Nightshade, Lancashire. Athenaeum 216, 17 Dec 1831, p. 816. Poem. [British Periodicals Collection, UMI]

Wilson, Professor. An Evening in Furness Abbey. Blackwoods Edinburgh Magazine 26:157, Sept 1829, P 540-560. Poem. [British Periodicals Collection, UMI]

Sketch-books of William Latham [no ref.] 1809 - 1823. Furness Abbey; Dalton-in-Furness Cross DP 291/56 18 Sep. 1817; 19 Sep. 1817. [LRO]

Account of Furness Abbey, in Lancashire. Universal Magazine of Knowledge and Pleasure 111, Sept 1802, p 153-156. [British Periodicals Collection, UMI]

18th Century

West, Thomas. A guide to the Lakes. 1778. [CCL]

The Antiquities of Furness: or, An Account of the Royal Abbey of St Mary, in the Vale of Nightshade, near Dalton in Furness. Monthly Review 52, Mar 1775, p222-229. Also in Westminster Magazine Oct 1774, p. 543. [British Periodicals Collection, UMI]

West, Thomas. The antiquities of Furness: or, an account of the Royal Abbey of St Mary in the Vale of Nightshade. Spilsbury, 1774. [CCL]

Plan of Furness Abbey by T West RCLJ 1/2/6 Undated. Presumably from his printed history. [LRO]

Buck's views of Furness abbey, etc. 1727-1728. DP 189 [LRO]

17th Century
Minister's accounts re the late Monastery of Furness. 1601. [CASB]
16th Century
Lordship of the late monastery of Furness. 1536-1538. Rent apportionments following dissolution. Z/109/6. [CASB].

Map of Furness Abbey possessions in Cumberland. 1537. ZK/198/4 [CASB]

Map of Furness Abbey possessions in Yorkshire and South Lonsdale. 1537. ZK/198/5. [CASB]

Furness Abbey rental, c 1530. Z/826/16 &17. Also ZK/205, rental for 1535-1537. [CASB]

Award, 30 Apr 1512(1) Alexander, Abbot of Furness Abbey, and the convent of the same....etc WDRY/1/3/8/3 & WDRY/1/3/8/4. [CASK]

15th Century and earlier
Copy Inspeximus, of the patent rolls of Henry V, reciting previous 17th C. charters of confirmation of Henry IV, Richard II and other royal charters, in regard to Furness Abbey, 1413-1414 (17th Century copy). WDRY 1/3/8/2. Including the foundation charter by Stephen, earl of Boulogne (later king of England). [CASK]

Chetham Society. Remains... New series, Vol. 94 : [Chetham miscellanies. Vol. 6.]. Manchester : C.S, 1935. Includes The Coucher book of Furness Abbey: transcript of the lost folio 70. [LCL]

Chetham Society. Remains... New series, Vol. 74, 76, 78 : The Coucher book of Furness Abbey : printed from the original manuscript in the British Museum, edited by John Brownbill, Vol 2. Manchester : C.S, [1915-1919] 3 volumes bound together. Titles of charters etc in English; text in Latin, with notes in English. Includes Index. [LCL]

Chetham Society. Remains... New series, Vol. 9, 11 & 14 : The Coucher book of Furness Abbey : printed from the original preserved in the Record Office London, edited by J.C. Atkinson. Vol. 1, Manchester : C.S, 1886-1888. 3 vols bound together. Titles of charters etc in English; text in Latin, with notes in English. Includes Index. [LCL]

The Henry Ogle Collection DDX 208 c14th century-1828 Scale drawings (many coloured) of glass, floor-tiles, churches, datestones, etc., including DDX 208/58 Capital of Early English period 13C Furness Abbey, Chapter House vestibule; DDX 208/71 Furness Abbey [LRO]

Licence to impark woods for Furness Abbey. 1338. Z/826/2. [CASB]

Pennington Manor: Mills v Muncaster: Documentary Evidence Vol V Pennington Manor. Includes several documents and charters concerning the manor and Abbey from Domesday Book onwards. Z/90. [CASB].

Extracts from Furness Cowcher Book, 1208-1652. Z/107. [CASB]

Furness Abbey. Translated transcript of Henry II Royal Charter confirming grant of lands to Furness Abbey. 1154. Z/109/2. [CASB]

Appendix 21

Other Lancashire monastic houses not included in this walk

Please see Appendix 1 - General Sources for full details of the main sources of information, and full references. The General Sources are not included below

Barnoldswick Abbey

Wright, Robert. '"Casting down the altars and levelling everything before the ploughshare"? The expansion and evolution of the grange estates of Kirkstall Abbey'. In Prestwich, Michael; Britnell, Richard Hugh; Frame, Robin (ed.), Thirteenth Century England IX : proceedings of the Durham Conference, 2001 (Woodbridge: Boydell, 2003), 187-200. ISBN 0851155758. Includes granges of Barnoldswick (Yorkshire) ; and Accrington (Lancashire)
[http://www.history.ac.uk/projects/bbih]
  Deeds relating to Barnoldswick and Gylkyrke, part of the lands of Kirkstall Abbey, 1345, 1563-1615, and copies of 2 early deeds (2). JC 234-1314 [Sheffield Archives]

Lytham Priory

Lytham Hall. Includes history: http://www.lythamhall.org.uk
Friends: http://www.lythamhall.org
  Durham. Cathedral Church of Christ and Saint Mary. [Calendar of extracts relating to Lytham mills from the account-rolls of Lytham Priory.]. Photocopies. The originals are in Durham Cathedral Library. [LCL]
  [KILGRIMOL : miscellaneous photocopies.]. Lost settlement - Priory - Lytham. A reputed lost settlement and priory off the coast of Lytham. [LCL]
  Foundation of Lytham Priory, [1336] - [1444]. Baines Manuscript Collection. Handwritten transcription. BAI C 72 11 [LCL]
  John Weld's sketch book DP 386/1 1830-1836. A book of pencil, ink and watercolour sketches by John Weld of Leagram Hall during the period c.1830-1886. The subjects are ancient monuments, churches and country houses in Lancashire. Page: 69 description: Lytham 3 location. The book also contains un-numbered pages with drawings of Lytham Hall. [LRO]
  Twenty charters belonging to Lytham Priory, 12th and 13th Centuries P/24 Undated Prof. G. Barraclough. 20 charters belonging to Lytham Priory 12C & 13C. Photocopies (early process!) of original charters, in Latin. Difficult to decipher (not sure whether they are all complete). Some transcriptions, in original Latin, but easier to read. [LRO]
  Lytham Priory, cell of Durham Cathedral Priory GB/NNAF/C16776 (Former ISAAR ref: GB/NNAF/O102387). DCD. [Durham University Library, Archives and Special Collections: Palace Green Section]
  15th cent: enrolled copies of 5 deeds 12th cent onwards. DL 41/101 [The National Archives].
  [Lytham Priory] Clifton of Lytham c1190-1939. Legal Papers: Re.... Butler v. Lytham priory 1531... DDLC [LRO]
  Microfilm copies of Documents held elsewhere. compoti 1310-1533. MF 1./1 Farrer transcripts of Lytham Priory deeds, vols 1 and 2. Handwritten, English 1274. Visitations 1347 Lytham: misc charters, c 1296 - 1600. Copies of charters handwritten and in Latin. Bond dates 1507, in English; to Thomas, Prior of monastery. Advowson of church of Appleby (1355), in English. Some others in English. [LRO]

Warrington Friars

Excavations at Warrington Friary 2000. Heawood, R. Publisher: Journal of the Chester Archaeological Society (JCAS) Volume 77 (for 2002). Year: 2003 [http://www.biab.ac.uk/contents/17778] [WL]

An Attempt to Identify the Boundaries of Warrington Friary Precinct From Documentary Sources. Wells, H. H. Wells, Warrington, Year: 2002 [WL]

Friary Dig. Heawood, Richard. In Warrington and District Archaeological and Historical Society Newsletter 32, Year: 2001. Report of his lecture to the Society on the excavation starting in December 1999 up to 2001, noting the earlier excavations of 1886, 1931 and 1978. Results of the dig and historical background on the friary. [WL]

Finally an item of local interest Rylance, Stephen. In Warrington and District Archaeological and Historical Society Newsletter 29, Year: 2000. Report from the Warrington Guardian Midweek 22 February 2000 on the unearthing of up to 30 bodies during the excavation of the Warrington Friary site prior to the construction of a Wetherspoon's public house. [WL]

Warrington Friary Wells, H., H. Wells, Warrington, Year: 2000. ISBN: 1901208036 [WL]

Austin Friars of Warrington Wells, Harry. Publisher: In Warrington and District Archaeological and Historical Society Newsletter 29, Year: 2000 [WL]

An Illuminated Manuscript From Warrington Friary. Wells, Harry "Lancashire History Quarterly" 2 (3), September, Year: 1998 [WL]

Christianity in Warrington From St Elphin to Robert Yates. Sellers, Ian. Publisher: Ian Sellers, Year: 1980 [WL]

A summary of the Warrington Friary excavations in 1978. Johnson, Barry. In Warrington and District Archaeological and Historical Society Newsletter 5, Year: 1979 [WL]

The Decorated Mosaic Tile Floor from Warrington Friary : A Re-assessment Greene, J Patrick. Publisher: Journal of the Chester Archaeological Society (JCAS) New Series, Volume 59, Year: 1976 [WL]

The Archaeology of Warrington's Past. Grealey, Shelagh. (director). Publisher: Warrington Development Corporation, PO Box 49, Warrington, Year: 1976 ISBN: 0950077739 [WL]

Chronological Data relating to the Churches of Cheshire Crossley, Fred H Transactions of the Lancashire & Cheshire Antiquarian Society (TLCAS), Volume 57 (for 1943/4), Year: 1946 [WL]

Warrington Friary : The Discoveries of 1931. Owen, Geoffrey & Cheetham, F H Transactions of the Historic Society of Lancashire & Cheshire (THSLC) Volume 88, Year: 1937 [WL]

Austin Friars, Warrington, Cheshire. Ground Plan. AL0265/114/03 25 Mar 1928 [EHNMR]

The Warrington Friary : the home of the Augustinian friars. Worsley, James Edwardson. In The Dawn Vol VIII pp 29-30, 46-7, 52-3, 82-4, 93, 119-20, 333-4, 142-4, Year: 1908 [WL]

Local Friaries and Priories. The Preston Chronicle (Preston, England), Saturday, February 14, 1891; Issue 4060 [LCLDL]

Warrington Friary and the Recent Discoveries There. Owen, William 'Transactions of the Historic Society of Lancashire and Cheshire' Volume XLI, pp 175-194.

Thomas Brakell, Liverpool, Year: 1890 [WL]

Warrington Friary: 1886 excavations. Photograph. [Warrington Museum: http://www.warringtonmuseum.co.uk.

History of Warrington Friary. Beamont, William (Editor) Chetham Society First Series Volume 83, Pub Year: 1872 [WL]

Archaeology in the Mersey district, 1870. Author: H. E. Smith. HSLC Volume: 23 (1870-1871) Pages: 119-152, illus. Includes information on remains possibly connected with Warrington priory. [LCL]

Leicester, Peter. An account of the Friary at Warrington. Baines Manuscript Collection. Handwritten copy of an extract from Sir Peter Leicester's "Antiquities of Cheshire". [LCL]

Grant of charters to Prior of Cockerham, Warrington; foundation of the Collegiate Church at Manchester; Lancaster (Black Friars); Preston (Grey Friars). Baines Manuscript Collection. Handwritten copy of extract from Dugdale's Monasticon. [LCL]

W Owen: plans of Warrington friary WMS 1005 [Cheshire Archives]

Ireland Blackburne of Hale 1203-1873. Title deeds: Warrington (Austin Friars) c. 1240-1780. [LRO]

Wyresdale Abbey

Cistercian Abbeys: Abington (Includes information about Wyresdsle). [http://cistercians.shef.ac.uk/abbeys/abington.php:]

Abbeystead in Wyresdale, and its endowed school. W. O. Roper. HSLC Vol 55 (1903-1904) Pages: 67-89, illus. Includes information on the abbey of Wyresdale. [LCL]

Grant by Theobald Walter to the abbey of Wyresdall of the town of Hamilton (or Hammondston), for the souls, etc. (as above.); Witnesses, Hubert, Archbishop of Canterbury, and others. MS 613, f. 21 No date. Former reference: MS 613, f. 21 Language: Latin. Grant by Theobald Walter, son of Hubert Walter, to the abbey of Wirisvalle (sic), of all his "haia" of Wirisvalle, for building there an abbey of the Cistercian order, who shall come from the house of Furness; the said abbey to be a daughter of Furness for ever. Witnesses named. [Lambeth Palace Library]

Grant by the same to the same of the town of Moreton. Grant by King Richard I. to Theobald Walter of Agemundernesse, etc. (as above.) Winchester, 22 April, 3 Ric. I. (Witnesses named.); Grant by Theobald Walter to the abbey of St. Mary, Wyresdall, of the church of St. Michael super Wyresdall, with its chapels, for the souls of Kings Henry [II.] and Richard [I.], of John Earl of Moreton, and Hubert, Archbishop of Canterbury, brother of said Thomas. Witnesses, various abbots and others. MS 613, f. 20 No date Former reference: MS 613, f. 20 Language: Latin Contents: Witnesses, Geoffrey de Perth and others. Dated at Portsmouth (Portsmuo). http://archives.lambethpalacelibrary.org.uk/CalmView/Record.aspx?src=CalmView.Catalog&id=MSS%2f596-638%2f613%2f20&pos=1 [Lambeth Palace Library]

Duchy of Lancaster: Deeds, Series L DL 25/3623 Wyresdale Abbey to H. the Chaplain: grant, indented, of the land on the east side of the church of St. Michael's (St. Michael on Wyre), with the fishery there: (Lancs). Wyresdale Abbey to H. the Chaplain: grant, indented, of the land on the east side Date range: 1100 - 1682. [National Archives]

Index